"A must-read for tweens in stepfamili[
these important members of the ste[
Stepfamily Foundation

"Perfectly describes the feelings and experiences that kids handle as a result of blended families. Includes hands-on exercises, heartfelt wisdom, and much needed humor. It's a must-have for every stepfamily wanting to create a sense of warmth, open communication, and love for their children." —RONI LEIDERMAN, PH.D., *Dean, Mailman Segal Institute for Early Childhood Studies, Nova Southeastern University*

"A much needed book for young teens living through family upheaval. Drawn from interviews with real stepkids, the authors help young readers identify and deal with their feelings and learn strategies for coping, while keeping a positive outlook that this, too, can be not only dealt with—but maybe even have some positive outcomes." —HARRIET HEATH, PH.D., *Director, The Parent Center, Child Study Institute and Thorne School, Bryn Mawr College*

How to Deal with Life in a STEPFAMILY

LISA COHN AND DEBBIE GLASSER, PH.D.
ILLUSTRATED BY STEVE MARK

free spirit
PUBLiSHiNG®

Helping kids
help themselves®
since 1983

Library of Congress Cataloging-in-Publication Data
Cohn, Lisa, 1957-
   The step-tween survival guide : how to deal with life in a stepfamily / by Lisa Cohn and Debbie Glasser ;
   illustrated by Steve Mark.
      p. cm.
Includes index.
   ISBN 978-1-57542-297-8
   1. Stepchildren—Family relationships—Juvenile literature. 2. Stepchildren—Life skills guides—Juvenile literature.
   3. Stepfamilies—Life skills guides—Juvenile literature. 4. Children of divorced parents—Family relationships—
   Juvenile literature. I. Glasser, Debbie. II. Mark, Steve, ill. III. Title.
   HQ777.7.C63 2008
   306.874'7—dc22
                                                        2008012062

The names of the young people quoted throughout the book have been changed to protect their privacy.

Edited by Meg Bratsch
Cover and interior design by Calico and Tilka Design

10 9 8 7 6 5 4 3 2 1
Printed in the United States of America

Free Spirit Publishing Inc.
217 Fifth Avenue North, Suite 200
Minneapolis, MN 55401-1299
(612) 338-2068
help4kids@freespirit.com
www.freespirit.com

Printed on recycled paper
including 30%
post-consumer waste

Free Spirit Publishing is a member of the Green Press Initiative, and we're committed to printing our books on recycled paper containing a minimum of 30% post-consumer waste (PCW). For every ton of books printed on 30% PCW recycled paper, we save 5.1 trees, 2,100 gallons of water, 114 gallons of oil, 18 pounds of air pollution, 1,230 kilowatt hours of energy, and .9 cubic yards of landfill space. At Free Spirit it's our goal to nurture not only young people, but nature too!

green
press
INITIATIVE

Dedication

This book is dedicated to my own stepfamily—Bill and all our kids—with love. —L.C.

Dedicated to Glenn, Emily, Ben, and Sam, the family I love, admire, and learn from every day. —D.G.

Acknowledgments

Thanks to the dozens of kids and teens living in stepfamilies who shared their stories with us. You are the heart of this book! We also appreciate your parents' willingness to arrange interviews with us. Thanks, too, to the adults who shared their stepfamily stories. You provide hope, a sense of humor, and inspiration. We also appreciated the feedback we received from Lisa's writing group in Portland, Oregon, as well as the expertise of Susan K. Dandes, Ph.D., Associate Professor of Clinical Pediatrics at the University of Miami Miller School of Medicine.

Thanks, especially, to Free Spirit Publishing Director John Kober and editors Douglas Fehlen and Meg Bratsch for your support and helpful feedback. It's a treat working with you!

We'd like to express our gratitude to the people who make up our big blended families and inspired us to write this book. They include our children, spouses, ex-spouses, ex-spouses' partners, parents, brothers, and sisters—and all the people they have brought into our children's lives.

Contents

Making the Best of a Not-So-Great Situation

Meet Jake. His parents are divorced and both of them recently remarried. Now he splits his time between his mom and stepdad's place and his dad and stepmom's place.

For Jake, living in stepfamilies has its pluses and minuses. On the positive side, his stepdad has changed Jake's life and Jake's mom's life for the better. He has brought love and a strong sense of family to their home. He offers to help Jake if he's having trouble with his schoolwork. He takes Jake to sports memorabilia shows and fun sporting events. He also tells Jake and Jake's brother that he cares about them and wants to be a positive influence in their lives.

However, over at Jake's dad's house, life isn't so rosy. Jake doesn't like his bossy stepmom, and he feels like his dad never backs him up when his stepmom tries to tell Jake what to do.

If you're reading this book, your parents are probably divorced and you're likely living at least part-time in a stepfamily, or maybe splitting your time between two stepfamilies. And, like Jake, you're probably dealing with lots of pluses and minuses.

What is a stepfamily?

The word "stepfamily" means a family made up of:

* you

* your parent

* your siblings (if you have any)

* your stepparent (the person your parent remarried or is living with)

* your stepsiblings (kids your stepparent may already have)

Maybe just one of your parents is remarried or lives with a partner, and your other parent lives alone, so you have only one stepfamily. Maybe both of your parents remarried or found new partners, and you are living in two stepfamilies— one at your mom's place and one at your dad's place. Or maybe your situation is even more complicated than that! Whatever your life may look like as a stepkid—this book is for you.

What is a blended family?

The word "stepfamily" is used in this book, but you might also sometimes hear the term "blended family." This is just another way of saying "stepfamily." It's about two families coming together and uniting — "blending." Don't get the idea, though, that family members should "blend" or combine all their possessions and spend every minute together. In all families, people like to have their own time and their own stuff once in a while.

Know your steps

stepmom: (noun) the woman your parent remarried or is living with

stepdad: (noun) the man your parent remarried or is living with

stepsibling: (noun) a kid your stepparent already had

stepcousin: (noun) your stepparent's niece or nephew

stepaunt: (noun) your stepparent's sister

stepuncle: (noun) your stepparent's brother

stepgrandparent: (noun) your stepparent's parent

stepdog/stepcat/stepfish/stephamster: (noun) take a wild guess!

Your stepmom might be trying to introduce you to vegetarian food, or may have moved the TV to the basement. You may barely even recognize your mom anymore, who's so in love with your stepdad she seems to have forgotten all about you. Meanwhile, your dad might be horrified that you now have a stepfather. He might be acting jealous and reminding you every day that he's your real dad and he's the one who woke up in the middle of the night to feed you as a baby.

Like many kids your age, there's a good chance you feel frustrated at times…as well as confused, angry, and lost. As a tween, you might feel caught between childhood and teenhood—too old for toys and kid stuff, but too young for teen stuff, like driving, dating, and being more independent. To make things worse, as a stepkid you might also feel caught between all the adults (and maybe even new siblings) in your life—not to mention between two separate homes.

In short: it can be tough enough being a stepkid, let alone a step-tween.

stepkid + tween = *step-tween*

step-tween: (noun) an open-minded, flexible but sometimes bewildered guy or girl roughly between the ages of 9 and 12 who lives in a stepfamily and is eager to learn how to make the most of it

The good news is: You're not alone. Currently, around 4.5 million stepkids under the age of 18 live in the United States, and close to that many in Canada. In fact, nearly 30 percent of all U.S. children are likely to spend some time in a stepfamily. Like you, they have lots of feelings as they deal with all the changes taking place in their family. Some of these feelings are happy. Some are not-so-happy.

Top Gripes from Step-Tweens

Here are common complaints from kids like you, based on interviews:

- 4.5 million stepkids currently live in the United States
- 30 percent of all U.S. children will spend time in a stepfamily

* My stepparent is bossy and tries to push new rules on me.

* It feels weird having strange stepsiblings and stepparents (or even stepdogs and stepcats!)—in my home.

* My stepparent favors his or her kids over me.

* My parent is always on my stepparent's side and doesn't support my point of view.

* My privacy feels invaded by my stepsibling, who now shares a room (or bathroom) with me.

* I want to spend more time alone with my real parent and siblings.

* My stepparent is jealous of my parent and me and competes with us.

* The new baby my parent and stepparent had gets all the attention.

How This Book Can Help You

In this book, you'll learn skills for surviving—and thriving—in your stepfamily. You'll gain lots of **Survival Tools** that help you think about your feelings and express them to people around you.

You'll also find **Know Yourself** quizzes that help you discover things about yourself—like how you react to situations and make decisions. You'll learn that you have many choices, even though it may sometimes feel like you have none. In the **Reality Check** sections, you get ideas for how to deal when nothing else seems to help. The **Stepping Closer** sections give you tips for getting to know your new family members better.

Along the way, you'll meet other stepkids, like Jake, who were interviewed for this book. They range in age from 8 to 16 and come from many different backgrounds and family situations. They share their own struggles and successes in the sections called **Stepkids Speak Out** and **Step-Tween Survival Tips**. When you read their stories, maybe you'll relate to some of their troubles.

You'll also read many positive stories. You'll learn how step-tweens have made their situations better, and have become stronger, happier, and healthier as a result of experiences that can be challenging at times.

Top Things Tweens Like About Living in Stepfamilies

* I have more people in my life to turn to.

* I get a break from one parent (or sibling) when I go to the other parent's home.

* I like being the one my younger stepsibling looks up to.

* I am learning a lot about how to deal with different kinds of people.

* It's fun having two homes and two families—which also means getting more gifts on holidays!

* I like my stepsiblings and wish I could see them more often.

* It's fun having such a big family.

As you hear other stepkids' stories, keep in mind that stepfamily life often begins with some bumps in the road. But in time, many tweens settle into their new family and grow to like—and even love—their new family members.

(By the way, a "new" family member might mean someone you've lived with for two months or a few years. It takes time for stepfamily members to get to know each other.)

How to Use This Book

Not everything in this book will apply to your situation. For example, you may not have stepsiblings, like some of the kids quoted in this book. You may not live in two different homes. But you can learn from other kids' challenges and how they dealt with tough situations.

Read the book all the way through or, if you prefer, skim the Contents and read the sections that interest you most.

You might want to keep a notebook to jot down ideas you have while reading, and to journal about events and feelings related to your own stepfamily life. You can title the notebook your "Survival Log." Use it to record your answers to the quizzes and other questions in the book (whenever you see the pencil icon).

As you're reading, the most important thing to remember is: although the tools in this book are for you—to help gain some control of your situation—you're not expected to face these changes on your own. It's up to parents, stepparents, and other trusted adults to provide the support, guidance, and understanding you need in order to adjust to stepfamily life.

Still, there are many things you can do. Even though you can't control the members of your stepfamily—such as how they feel, what they say, how they eat, dress, or decorate their bedrooms—you can control *your* behavior. You are in charge of the words that come out of your mouth (that sometimes should stay there!). You're also in charge of how you act, how you express your feelings, and how you ask for help and support.

Read on to learn how to express yourself, handle new situations, and reach out to others in ways that not only help you survive, but *thrive*, in your stepfamily.

We'd like to hear your story and how this book helps you. We'd also like to know if you have any questions or want to find out more. You can email us at help4kids@freespirit.com or send a letter to us in care of:

Free Spirit Publishing

217 Fifth Avenue North, Suite 200

Minneapolis, MN 55401-1299

Don't forget to include your address, so we can write back to you. Good luck in your stepfamily adventures.

Lisa Cohn & Debbie Glasser

CHAPTER 1

How to Deal with All Those Strong, Surprising, or Confusing Feelings

As a step-tween, you probably experience a wide range of feelings. Sometimes all these feelings can be mixed together at once. Needless to say, it can get a little confusing.

In this chapter, you'll learn that other stepkids experience many of the emotions that you may be feeling about your family. You'll also get ideas for expressing your feelings in ways that may help others understand you better.

Stepkids Speak Out

When I was little, I remember that I used to cry and cry when my parents yelled and fought. —ZIAD

It's fun to live in a stepfamily. It's kind of exciting going back and forth. You have two houses and you get two bedrooms and two families and stuff like that. —PAIGE

When I found out I was going to have a baby sister, I was worried, wondering what would happen. I didn't really know what it would be like to have a sister. At first, she got a lot of attention. My aunt would play with her a lot, and that made me feel a little jealous. —LINDSAY

Four Things You Might Feel— Maybe All at Once

1. Sadness

You might feel sad about the family life you used to have. Even if your parents argued a lot when they were married, you still may miss the feeling of being together.

2. Anger

Maybe your parents are saying negative things about each other in front of you. Maybe they're not even talking to each other and are expecting you to send messages between them. You might feel caught in the middle and angry. You might also be upset with one or both of your parents for breaking up the family.

3. Fear

If one (or both) of your parents remarries or starts living with a new partner, it may mean you'll have to move to a new neighborhood and leave your friends behind. You may have to share a room with a stepsibling you hardly know. One of your parents may even be having a new baby. Facing the unknown can be scary.

4. Happiness:

There can be plenty of things to feel happy about in a stepfamily. You might have a new stepparent who really cares about you. Your new stepsister may turn out to be the sister you've always wanted but never had before. You may feel excited and hopeful about your new family life.

Chances are, you're experiencing all these feelings and more in your stepfamily. You may feel embarrassed about your parents' remarriage or new partnership, confused about whether you like your stepparents, or jealous of your stepsiblings. You may also feel relieved that your parents don't argue like they used to.

Your emotions may change from day to day, hour to hour, even minute to minute. You might find yourself feeling both angry and afraid at the same time, or both happy and sad. Of course, some emotions are easier to cope with than others.

cope: (verb) to deal with difficulties—successfully!

Survival Tool #1: Let 'Em Out!

One of the best ways to cope with difficult feelings is to get them out of your head and out in the open. Let 'em out! Try talking about your feelings with a friend, parent, teacher, or counselor. Try expressing them on paper—in a drawing or poem or song lyrics. You might even create a painting or sculpture that captures your mood. Physical activity (like dancing or playing sports) can be a great way to "let 'em out," too. The possibilities are endless. The key is to figure out which style feels most comfortable for you.

Know Yourself: How Do You Let 'Em Out?

Here's a quiz to help you find the best way for you to cope with strong feelings.

1. **A TV producer is in your city looking for kids to star in several new "reality TV" shows. Which show would you be most likely to audition for?**
   a) Triathlon: Battle of the All-Star Athletes
   b) The Score: Who Will Be the New Beethoven?
   c) Novel Discoveries: In Search of the Next Great Novelist
   d) Under One Roof: Eight Friends, Seven Days, and No Break from Each Other

2. **It's the weekend and you have no plans. The first thing you reach for is:**
   a) Your bicycle
   b) Your CD or MP3 player
   c) Your journal or sketch pad
   d) Your phone to call a friend

3. **If you could switch lives with one of the adults at your school for a day, whose job seems the most fun and interesting?**
   a) The gym teacher
   b) The band director
   c) The art teacher
   d) The school psychologist

4. **You really enjoy:**
   a) Working up a sweat
   b) Working on new dance steps
   c) Working with your hands
   d) Working on your social life

If you answered "a" for most questions, you're a kid in action! Sports and other high-energy activities may be a great way for you to let off steam and let out your feelings. Go ahead and kick that soccer ball or get out that snowboard. Just remember: It's great to exercise, but try not to do it instead of talking about your feelings (when you really need to talk).

If "b" was your choice most of the time, you've got the music in you. Dancing, playing, or listening to music may be an ideal way for you to cope with big feelings. Sing along with your favorite songs (karaoke, anyone?), dance to a favorite tune in the privacy of your room…or onstage in front of an audience. Learn how to play the guitar, piano, violin—anything. If you express yourself through music, go for it. But also make time to share your feelings in other ways. Your family and friends might not be able to hear what you're trying to tell them over that thumping bass line!

Did you choose "c" a lot? You're an artist at heart. Expressing yourself creatively might be what you were born to do. Feeling sad? Pick up your

watercolors and express your "blue" mood. Feeling hopeful? Write about it in your journal. The key to artistic expression is to recognize your true feelings and put them into words on paper or colors on canvas. Remember this: Even artists reach out to others. So look up from your sketchpad once in a while and talk with the people in your life who want to hear from you.

If "d" was usually your choice, it's probably safe to say you're a "people person." Chances are, you're someone who feels comfortable around people and can talk to others easily. It's also likely that you've got a solid audience of listeners in your life. If socializing is your Let 'Em Out style, go ahead and share your feelings. Just remember to share them with people you know and trust. You don't want to spill your innermost feelings to every kid in math class.

Now you have some idea about how you tend to express your emotions. What do other stepkids have to say about letting out their feelings?

Step-Tween Survival Tips

I'm a painter. When I was first in a stepfamily, I spent a lot of time on my artwork. Have a creative outlet, or sport, or a passion. Find a place for you to let out the energy. —ANNA

You will get through it. Focus on something you love to do. For me, I loved to write and I stayed as creative as possible. —JONATHAN

Communication is number one. Whatever kind of feelings you're having, it's okay to communicate them. —MORGAN

Reality Check:
When Letting 'Em Out Is Not Enough

Let's say you're spending a lot of time letting out your feelings by playing basketball, dancing, painting, writing, or chatting with friends. But the truth is, you may still be pretty sad, frustrated, or upset. See Survival Tool #2 below for an idea of how to deal.

Survival Tool #2:
Talk with an Adult You Trust

Reach out to an adult you trust and tell him or her how you feel. Talk to a parent or stepparent, aunt, uncle, grandparent, teacher, coach, religious leader, or counselor. Don't keep those feelings inside. Help is available! You might begin by saying something like, "I'm spending a lot of time writing about my new stepfamily. It helps, but not enough. Could I talk to you about it?"

Stepping Closer

Have you ever had a tough conversation with a friend, and then felt closer after you talked it out? One way to step closer to a stepsibling is to let your feelings out. It may feel uncomfortable at first, but if you can talk about what's on your mind, you'll feel more connected to him or her. For example, if you hate the TV shows your stepsister watches constantly in your shared room, find a way to talk about it. Be sure to leave time to hear her point of view. Also, remember that she's a stepkid just like you (she might even have a "second home" with her other parent), and she's probably facing a lot of the same challenges you are.

CHAPTER 2

You Want to Explain Your Feelings, But How?

Step-Tween Survival Tips

As much as you can, talk about how things are making you feel. You'll be in much better condition than letting things go and getting angry. Getting angry isn't going to solve anything. —*KAT*

You need to stick up for yourself and what you want. Communicate, communicate, communicate! —*ETHAN*

Kat and Ethan give great advice about the importance of communication. But here's the thing: Talking about your feelings in a stepfamily can be very different from sharing your feelings in a family you've been in your whole life.

Why It's Hard to Communicate in a Stepfamily at First

1. You don't know the "rules" yet

Every family has its own beliefs about how and when to share feelings. These are the "rules" the family lives by, and they are not always obvious or clear. The fact is, you're still learning the "rules" of your new family. You probably don't know enough about your stepfamily members yet to know whether you can tease them, laugh at them, cry around them, or be straight with them. It can be really easy at first to break the "rules" without even realizing it.

2. You may feel out of control

When you're part of a stepfamily, it's normal to feel a little—or a lot—out of control at first. It's like learning a new sport or activity, where you don't know what to expect next. You may not know what to do or say, or when to do or say it. You might feel like what you want doesn't matter to those around you. You might feel like you're no longer in charge of your own life.

Maybe you clam up when you feel this way. Or maybe you talk nonstop, but you don't reveal your true feelings. Or maybe you try to figure out what the people around you want to hear, and you say that. All these ways of feeling and acting are understandable.

3. It's hard to be open with people you don't trust yet

Getting to know the members of your new family will take time. You may not trust them yet. It may be difficult—and even scary—to open up to them right away.

4. Strong feelings aren't always easy to share

When you're having a hard time figuring out the new family rules, you can experience some really strong feelings. Take Chloe, for example. Her dad remarried a year after her mom died. A whole new family moved into her house. She had to share her room with a new stepsister who had completely different tastes in music, clothes, and decorating.

"All of a sudden, there was nowhere in my own home where I could have privacy," says Chloe. She was really angry and sad. She didn't know how to talk about her feelings or who to turn to.

This chapter helps you learn all kinds of ways to communicate your feelings to others—without losing your cool. To begin, take a look at how you usually communicate, at your "say-it" style. Do you pour out whatever is in your heart? Do you hide your feelings and hope people will read your mind? Choose the answer that best applies to you for the following question.

Know Yourself: What's Your "Say-It" Style?

Your stepmom announces she wants you to clean your room once a week while she supervises. What do you do?

a) Yell at her, "You're not my mother and you can't tell me what to do!"

b) Agree to everything she says, then sit in your room and think about how much you hate her.

c) Tell her, "I know you're trying to be helpful, but can we talk about this new rule?"

If you answered "a," you may be someone who usually says whatever's on your mind. Chances are, you express yourself with a lot of feeling—but without thinking about the possible consequences.

The good news	*The not-so-good news*
You're probably a very honest and open person. Everyone around you knows how you feel.	This style can make others feel uncomfortable. Your spew-it-all style might hurt the feelings of the people you're trying to talk to. This can make it difficult for them to listen to you or help you work out a solution.

→

If you answered "b," you may really like to please others.
You probably get uncomfortable when people argue with each other.

The good news	*The not-so-good news*
You want to get along. You're likely to work hard to understand other people's points of view and to make them happy.	You may have a tendency to hide your feelings, which can make you feel angry at times. Even though you're trying to keep your anger under wraps, it doesn't disappear. In a stepfamily, this can really confuse the people who don't know you very well. You say you're "fine," but you act upset anyway.

If "c" was your answer, you may be a Straight Talker (see Survival Tool #3 on the following page). You have a calm, direct style of getting your point across. You let out your feelings in a way that makes other people want to listen to you. People around you may even want to help improve your situation.

The good news	*The not-so-good news*
You have an unusual talent! This is an effective way of communicating that can take some practice to learn. It can be very useful in a stepfamily, and throughout your life.	Even if you're a Straight Talker, some issues can be so touchy that the other person may have a difficult time listening to you. And if you're too direct, you can offend the person you're trying to communicate with. You may still end up feeling frustrated, disappointed, or angry.

Survival Tool #3: Practice Straight Talk

Straight Talk is a style of communicating that enables you to make a point or ask for something you need in a respectful and calm manner. In other words, it's talking without yelling. It's sticking to the point so people will listen to what you have to say. Often, it's a great way to help you get what you want!

Communicate, Communicate, Communicate!

Now that you're more familiar with your own "say-it" style, keep this style in mind as you read about some of the stepkid problems in this book. Consider whether your way of talking helps you get what you want or simply causes a lot of trouble. You might not be a Straight Talker yet, but don't be too hard on yourself. Remember: It's not easy to be a good communicator, especially when you're suddenly living with people you hardly know. Be patient, go easy on yourself, and keep trying. Learning new skills like Straight Talk takes time.

Six Tips for Using Straight Talk

Once you decide to start using Straight Talk, practice these six tips to use it like a pro.

1. Take a breather

When you feel yourself getting frustrated or angry in a situation, take 10 seconds to just breathe and think. The quickest way to get yourself into trouble is to start talking without thinking about what you're saying. Everyone has strong feelings sometimes, and it's natural to want to express them. But letting loose strong emotions without considering the consequences can be hurtful to others and may do more harm than good.

2. Set a goal

While you're taking a 10-second breather, think about your goal. What do you want to communicate? Let's say your stepdad announces he wants to store some boxes and old furniture in your bedroom. Before he ruins your space, take a few minutes to think about what you want to say to him. Once you've figured this out, you'll be more likely to make your point clearly and work on reaching a solution.

3. Know who you're talking to

Before you start reacting to a situation—even just using body language like rolling your eyes or crossing your arms—consider who you are talking to. Does this person have a short temper? Does this person know you well? Is he or she open to jokes?

For example, if the person you are talking to is your best friend, go ahead and roll your eyes. (Your friend is probably used to it!) But maybe you're talking to your new stepdad and he's asking you for the fifth time to take out the trash. You'll probably want to resist the temptation to roll your eyes and cross your arms—such body language tends not to go over too well with adults.

4. Stay in the present

Let's say your stepmom wants you to do a better job of picking up the stuff (jacket, hat, backpack) that you drop in the hallway when you come home from school. She wants everything put away immediately—before you have a snack, call your friend, or watch TV.

Your best bet is to stick to the facts in the present time. Avoid saying things like, "You always treat me like a baby," or "You never listen." Words like "always" and "never" usually make you—and the person you're talking too—angrier, and they usually aren't true. (Is it really true that your stepmom *never* listens?) Also avoid bringing up past issues that have already been resolved, like "This is just like that time you made me clean my room right when I got home."

Instead, you might try something more direct, like, "I'd like to talk about me picking up my stuff in the hall." Your stepmom will be more likely to listen, and you'll be more likely to make your point without making a scene.

5. Stay calm

When using Straight Talk, expressing yourself calmly can definitely work to your advantage. You might even try repeating a word or phrase in your head to help you stay focused. "Chill" and "Keep it together" are some popular ones.

Sure, yelling and screaming might feel good—it can be a relief to get angry feelings off your chest. But the relief you get doesn't last long. Yelling usually only leads to more yelling, more headaches, and sometimes to tough consequences, like the loss of a privilege. (See Chapter 1 for good ways to let out your feelings.)

6. Use I-messages

When using Straight Talk, try to begin your sentences with "I" to explain how you feel: "I feel mad that…" Avoid using You-statements that may start arguments, for example, "You are making me mad."

Survival Tool #4:
Use I-Messages

As you probably guessed, I-messages are not the same as instant messages (IMs) that you send online. Instead, they're a powerful way to get your thoughts, needs, and ideas across when you're experiencing strong feelings or want to make a point. They can help you express both positive and negative emotions. If you begin your sentence with "I" and explain how you feel, your listeners are more likely to hear you. If you begin a statement with "You" and accuse your listeners of doing or saying something wrong, they may be less likely to hear you or understand how you feel.

Examples of I-messages

* *"I feel upset that we don't have much time for just the two of us anymore. I miss spending time alone with you."*

* *"I get angry when my stepmom tells me when I should go to bed. Dad, would you sit down and talk with me about how to help her understand how I feel?"*

Examples of You-messages

* *"You are too picky for wanting me to clean my room all the time."*

* *"You can be so bossy when you tell me how to behave at the dinner table."*

Think about why using You-messages like these might make someone tune out and not get you the results you want. Remember, I-messages are a great way to express positive feelings, too.

Examples of positive I-messages

* *"I am happy that you, dad, and Julie are all coming to my school play. That means a lot to me."*

* *"I feel better now around my stepdad after we talked about how he acts at my soccer games."*

Think of things you would like to express to the people in your life, beginning your sentences with "I." Take a few minutes to write them in your Survival Log.

Straight Talk in Action

While using Straight Talk won't magically resolve every tough situation, it is usually a wise place to start. To practice, look at some real-life stepfamily situations.

 Stepkids Speak Out

My stepdad tries to push "family game night" on us. But I'd rather be with my friends. —JAKE

Family Game Night

If you were in Jake's shoes and wanted to use Straight Talk, what would you do?

a) Shout at your stepdad: "You're not the boss of me!" and storm out of the house.

b) Tell your stepdad, "I know game night is important, but I also like to hang out with my friends. When I have plans with friends, could we plan game night for another night?"

c) Tell your friends you can't go to the movies because it's family game night. Then, sulk in your room and think about how much you wish your stepdad never entered your life.

Yep, you guessed it—option "b" is the Straight Talk response.
You tell your stepdad how you feel without slamming doors or stewing alone with your anger. It may even help you two move closer to working out a solution and getting along better.

Stepkids Speak Out

My new stepsister, who shared my room with me, plastered the walls with ugly puppy dog posters. I didn't feel at home in my own room. —CHLOE

Sharing a Room

If you were Chloe, what would be your best Straight Talk response?

a) Tell your stepsister, "I'm glad you want to decorate the walls. I do, too. How about we go to the mall together and choose some posters that we both really like?"

b) Say nothing to your stepsister about the posters. Then, insult her decorating taste behind her back.

c) Shout at your stepsister, "Those posters are the stupidest things I've ever seen! How can you even look at them?"

As you probably guessed, "a" is the answer most likely to lead to a peaceful conversation, a fun day at the mall, and maybe even some cool new wall art.

A Few Good Things About Straight Talk

Just in case you're still not sold on Straight Talk, here's a list of four big pluses:

+ Straight Talk often gets you what you want.

Whether you'd like a night out alone with your mom or a new desk for your bedroom, speaking calmly and respectfully is your best bet for making these wishes come true.

+ It works outside of stepfamilies, too.

You can use Straight Talk with teachers, coaches, and even friends. Straight Talk can help you resolve arguments, get things done, and express yourself better in many areas of life. It may even help you communicate your ideas more clearly in writing and improve your grade in English class!

+ It makes everyday problems seem easier.

It's simple: If you talk about your troubles in an honest, straightforward, and polite way, people respond better to your day-to-day concerns. You are communicating your feelings in a way people can understand, so they will be more likely to listen to you.

+ It will help you earn respect from others.

People will respect you for being brave and honest enough to express your feelings, even when it's difficult. Tweens who have the guts to express their feelings gain respect and often are seen as leaders.

Step-Tween Survival Tips

At our house, we keep a toy microphone at the dinner table. At dinner time, one person gets to hold the microphone and say whatever they want to say. Everyone listens. Then we pass it to the next person. This is a good way to get stuff off your chest and explain how you feel. —*PAIGE*

Reality Check: When to Call for Backup

No matter how hard you try to use Straight Talk and I-messages, sometimes you need extra help expressing yourself. That's normal. For example, you've tried to explain to your stepdad how you feel about family game night, but he still thinks you're being difficult and "antisocial." Try talking to your mom or a stepsibling, who may be more used to dealing with your stepdad than you are. They may be more understanding of your position and willing to back you up when talking to your stepdad. They might even be able to give you some pointers on how best to communicate with him.

Stepping Closer

Even when you're not getting along with stepparents or stepsiblings, you may notice something you really like about them. Maybe your stepbrother is really good with his two dogs. Or you like how your stepmom has rearranged the living room. When you notice such positives—share them! Tell your stepbrother, "You really seem to have a connection with animals. Your dogs just adore you." Tell your stepmom, "You have a very creative way of making rooms look better. How did you learn to do that?" Giving such compliments can help you feel closer to your stepfamily members—even during tense times. And they will likely appreciate your kind words.

CHAPTER 3

How to Handle Stepparent Troubles

Before her dad married Susan, Kat stayed up late most nights watching TV and ate whatever she wanted for dinner—which was pretty much junk food. Then her new stepmom came along and started changing all the rules. Susan wanted Kat to have a regular bedtime and she began serving green vegetables like asparagus and Brussels sprouts with every meal.

"In my mind I'm thinking, 'Who do you think you are? You aren't a parent and you aren't my parent,'" says Kat.

Another step-tween, Olivia, doesn't like it when her new stepdad disciplines her. Whenever Olivia's mom tries to discipline, her stepdad gets involved, too.

"He's pretty strict," Olivia says. "I wish he wouldn't get into it at all. He tries to replace my real dad and doesn't know how to act around me."

So here you are in a stepfamily, with a new stepparent, and probably some new rules, expectations, and styles of discipline. Like Olivia, you might be upset if your new stepdad tells you how to behave, especially if he's stricter than your mom. Like Kat, you may be annoyed if your stepmom wants you to eat strange-looking vegetables for dinner every night.

If you're feeling confused or upset about the changes in your life, that's normal.

Most kids don't appreciate someone new coming into their home and telling them what to do. When stepparents act this way, it can create some tough situations. It can also create sour feelings between you and your stepparent, between your stepparent and your parent, and even between your parent and you.

There are many ways you can choose to handle stepparent troubles like the ones Kat and Olivia face. Some of them will help you get what you want and need. Some of them won't. This chapter offers ideas for dealing successfully with sticky stepparent situations. You'll also read about some common tween ways of dealing that generally won't get you what you want. For instance, screaming at your stepmom, "You're not my mother!" will likely hurt her feelings and probably won't work out so well for you.

 ## Stepkids Speak Out

It used to make me angry when my stepmom tried to act like my parent. I said, "You're not my mom" a few times, but then I thought about how rude it was.
—ZIAD

Six Things You Can Do When Your Stepparent Goes Overboard with Rules

Here are some tips from stepkids who've been there about what to do when your stepparent goes overboard with discipline or new rules.

1. Try to understand what's going on

It may be annoying when your new stepparent tells you when to go to bed or what to eat. That's understandable. But is your stepparent purely a mean person who wants to ruin your life? Probably not. Often, when stepparents try to act like your parent, it's their way of showing you they care.

For example, take Kat's vegetable-and-bedtime obsessed stepmom, Susan. For just a minute, let's give her a break and consider her point of view. Like Kat, Susan's in a family that's completely new to her. She sees stuff happening that she thinks is wrong, and maybe even bad for her stepdaughter (like eating junk food and staying up until midnight).

Serving healthy food and helping Kat get more sleep is probably Susan's way of saying she cares about her.

Once Kat understands that Susan's just trying to be a caring stepmom, she might feel better. However, she still might think Susan's moving too fast and trying too hard. How can their problems be solved? Read on.

2. Talk to your stepparent about it

Kat could choose to share her feelings with her stepmom directly. If you choose to talk to a stepparent, remember to start on a positive note, like, "I know you're probably just trying to do the right thing." That will keep the situation from getting even stickier.

Straight Talk with Stepparents—
When your stepmom tries to set a new bedtime rule

Scene: *Your stepmom says, "You need to go to bed by 9:30."*

If you say: "You have no right to boss me around!"
She may: feel hurt and angry, and be unwilling to change her mind.

If you say: "I know you're trying to be a good stepmom, but I'm having a hard time with this new rule and I'd like to talk about it."
She may: decide to listen.

If you say: "I don't get tired until later and this early bedtime is hard for me because I'm not ready to fall asleep yet."
She may: begin to understand where you're coming from.

If you say: "Can we change my bedtime gradually, so I can get used to it?"
She may: surprise you by responding in a positive way.

3. Go to your parent for help

Sometimes, talking with a stepparent may not be easy or successful. Kat could choose instead to go directly to her dad for help. Remember: there are no right or wrong answers here.

Straight Talk with Parents About Stepparents—
Talking to your dad about your stepmom's bedtime rules

Scene: *Your stepmom says, "You need to go to bed by 9:30." You don't feel comfortable talking to her about it, so you decide to talk to your dad.*

If you say: "Dad, I hate your new wife and I wish you had never married her."
He may: feel hurt and angry, and be unwilling to help you.

If you say: "Dad, I'm sure Susan means well when she tells me to go to bed at 9:30. But I feel like some of her rules are too strict and I'm really having a hard time. I'm wondering if you can help me with this."

He may: be open to listening to you and decide to help you out.

He may even: agree to sit down with you and your stepmom to work out a solution.

4. Live with it—if it's reasonable

Maybe Kat decides she doesn't mind having a regular bedtime all that much. And she starts to think the freaky green vegetables aren't so bad, especially if she asks Susan to mix in her favorite veggies, like carrots and potatoes. Kat knows her stepmom isn't being unreasonably strict. She discovers it's not the rules that she minds—it's the fact that Susan is trying to act like her mom.

In fact, many tweens worry that if stepparents act too much like their mom or dad, they can somehow take the place of their parents. Even if your stepparent is involved in making decisions about your bedtime or what's on the dinner table, it doesn't mean he or she is replacing your mom or dad. It may be helpful to view your stepparent as a new adult in your home who is now part of your family.

If the new rules don't feel like prison sentences and aren't cramping your style too much, take a step back. Once in a while, you might give your stepparent a chance to look out for your best interests. Let him or her help you out, offer suggestions, and provide you with care and support. This may help both of you feel more like you're part of the same family.

5. Look for the positives

See Survival Tool #5 on the following page.

Survival Tool #5: Look for the Positives

Another possibility is that Kat even starts to *like* the fact that Susan is introducing new rules. She might begin to see that eating well and getting more sleep make her feel better and less tired throughout the day. Be on the lookout for ways that some of your stepparent's new rules or ideas might actually be changing your life for the better.

Stepkids Speak Out

Before my mom was with David, we lived in a messy house and I didn't do my homework. My mom always tried to discipline us, but never followed through. When David came into the family, my grades got better. He checked my homework. —JAKE

6. Share your feelings with someone

You might be feeling sad or confused or angry about having a new adult living in your home and taking part in your life. You may worry that your real parent will be jealous of your relationship with your stepparent. These are common feelings. Talk with other kids in stepfamilies, and with a teacher, a counselor, or other trusted adult about how you feel.

Lots of kids like their stepparents. You may, someday, too— if you don't already.

You may discover you're successful at handling tricky stepparent stuff by talking about it. Or you may find you need additional help. Either way, there's a good chance you'll come to love and trust your stepparent, whether it's in a few months or a few years. After all, there must be a reason your mom or dad fell in love with this person, right? If you keep an open mind, maybe you'll see those good qualities, too.

Stepkids Speak Out

My stepmom is a wonder woman. She is always very supportive of my choices. She listens to me and gives her opinions. She sits me down and asks me how I feel. She helps me think of ways to communicate better with my mom and stepdad. —TAYLOR

My stepdad always told me, "I'm not here to replace your dad, but to help you grow as a person and to take care of your mother." I never worried about him taking the place of my dad. —JAKE

Step-Tween Survival Tip

If you're having a hard time with a stepparent, be honest. If it's a problem you think can be fixed, go to your parent. Confront the issue right away. Then talk to your stepparent. Be as calm and respectful as you can. Focus on getting your feelings out so your stepparent knows how he's affecting you. _—TAYLOR_

Reality Check:
When to Ask for Help

Let's say you've thought about your stepparent's reasons for introducing new rules. You've tried talking with both your parent and stepparent to come up with solutions. You've used all your Straight Talk tips. And through it all, you didn't roll your eyes once! But nothing seems to be working. You may still be feeling sad, stressed, confused, or overwhelmed.

First, it's important to realize that while talking respectfully and openly can make it easier to get along with others, it's not a magic trick. It's simply a way of communicating that enables you to express your feelings in a way that makes it easier for the listener to understand you.

However, your best efforts might still not get you what you want. If that's the case, instead of giving up or yelling to make your point—ask for help.

Suggest to your parent or stepparent that it might be helpful if you talked with a counselor, so you and your family can learn new ways to communicate and get along. If that doesn't work, talk to your school counselor or someone at your place of worship. You may also decide to confide in another trusted adult in your life, such as a teacher, aunt, uncle, or grandparent. You might say, "I'm having some trouble with something at home. My stepdad set all these new rules that I don't like, but I don't seem to be getting anywhere talking to him or my mom. Could I talk to you about it?"

Step-Tween Survival Tip

When I talk to a therapist, my ideas don't change. But talking to someone does help me put things in perspective. I can look at things from both sides. Instead of trying to get even with my stepdad, I try to work things out. —*OLIVIA*

Stepping Closer

Do you and your stepdad both have an interest in cars? Ask him some questions about pistons or pack mufflers. Do you love baseball just as much as your stepmom? Ask her about the time she saw Nolan Ryan pitch a no-hitter. Not only will you gain knowledge about a hobby you enjoy, you may also learn something new about your stepparent's interests and talents—which he or she is probably eager to share with you. Once you connect with each other in this way, chances are you'll both feel more trusting and understanding. Your stepparent may even loosen up on some of the new rules.

CHAPTER 4

Missing Your Old Family and Getting to Know Your New One

Stepkids Speak Out

The hardest part of the whole divorce was the new families, getting used to new people. That's a whole new family you have to deal with. —JORGE

I wish my dad would come back and my stepdad and stepsister would go away. —NICOLE

My stepmom picks me up from school every day, and I spend about three hours with her. She's always busy with the baby. She never plays with me like my mom does. —LINDSAY

Like Nicole and Jorge, you didn't ask for your parents to get divorced or remarried. Living with a stepparent and stepsiblings probably was not at the top of your "To Do" list.

You probably also miss your old family, just as Lindsay does. You may be having a hard time with the fact that you're spending time with a stepparent, when you're really missing your parent.

It's important to remember that you didn't create this scenario. It wasn't your choice and it's not your fault. There was nothing you could have done to prevent your parents from getting divorced, remarrying, or moving in with a new partner.

You didn't ask for this situation…yet here you are in the middle of it. If you're thinking about how much you miss your old family, give yourself time to treasure the memories and to share your feelings about this big change in your life.

You'll learn ways in this chapter to cope with the fact that your family isn't the same as it used to be. You'll also get some ideas for adjusting to your new family and identifying what's positive about it.

Stepkids Speak Out

If you go to one parent's, you miss the other parent. And if you go to that parent's, you miss the other one. You're always missing someone. —PAIGE

Five Things to Do If You Miss the Way Your Family Used to Be

1. Put a photo of your absent parent in your bedroom

Even though you're no longer living with both of your parents under one roof, you're still all part of the same family, and that won't change.

2. Stay connected to the parent you see least often

You can still stay close to the parent you don't live with regularly. You could ask the parent you do live with to help arrange regular email, instant message, or phone dates with your other parent.

3. Let yourself feel sad, angry, or scared

It's normal to have strong feelings after your parents get divorced or remarried. You might feel sad, angry, lonely, and scared all in the same day. Don't be hard on yourself if you feel these things. Instead, remember that you're human and you're allowed to experience all kinds of emotions. Don't pretend these feelings don't exist or try to push them away. The first step to feeling better is recognizing how you're feeling to begin with.

4. Grab a sketchbook, a guitar, or a basketball

Express your feelings. Draw, paint, write poetry, keep a journal, play sports, or create music. Let out your feelings in a way that feels safe and comfortable, so you don't have to hold them inside. Revisit Chapter 1 for more tips on expressing your feelings.

5. Talk to kids who've been there

Remember, a third of all kids in the United States will spend time in a stepfamily. So you're definitely not alone! Chances are you have friends or relatives who share some of your feelings and experiences. You might want to form your own "stepfamily support group" made up of several kids. Perhaps with the help of your parent, stepparent, or school counselor, find a time and place to meet with this group. Ask the other kids how they feel, if they miss their old family, and what they do to deal with their feelings. You'll be surprised how much better you feel simply by sharing your story with others in a similar situation.

Step-Tween Survival Tip

It's really helpful to have friends who will listen to you. It makes you feel better to talk. —*OLIVIA*

Survival Tool #6: Keep a Sense of Humor

Whenever you can, try to find the humor in your situation and make time to laugh. Laughter is a great way to let off steam and put things in perspective. You might read a comic novel or watch a funny movie about an "oddball" family or stepfamily (there are plenty of such films to choose from!). Or maybe you have home movies of your own family from when you were younger. If so, ask your parents and siblings to watch them with you. Share funny stories with each other about past vacations, holidays, birthdays, or other family events. If you feel like it, you might even share some of your "old" family stories, videos, or photos with your new stepfamily members, so they can get a laugh, too.

Be Patient

While you're trying out these tips, give yourself lots of time to get used to your new family. Forming a stepfamily doesn't happen overnight. It takes some family members a while to begin to feel like they know each other. There often are bumps in the road. Remember: Great things don't happen right away. Think about how long it takes you to figure out where you belong as a member of a new sports team. How many months or years does it take to learn to play the piano? How long does it take to become best friends with someone?

Take a minute to think about what happens quickly in your life, and what's worth waiting for.

Things that happen quickly

* Receiving or sending an email or instant message

* Ordering at a fast food restaurant

* Laughing at a funny joke

* Getting a pimple on your chin the morning of the school dance

* Shivering when it's cold outside

Things that take more time

* Forming a winning soccer team

* Finding a true best friend

* Learning a new skill, like playing an instrument or cooking a meal

* Feeling like you "belong" in your new neighborhood

* Getting to know your stepfamily

Notice that you often experience the "Things that happen quickly" for a short period of time, like eating the fast food you ordered or reading an IM from your friend. You don't often remember them for very long.

Finding friends, being part of a group, learning a new skill—these are experiences that take longer and you don't easily forget. The "Things that take more time" often require you to work hard and be patient. You usually have to make lots of mistakes and feel out of place for a little while until these things start to feel "right."

Seeing the Best in Your New Family

At the beginning of this chapter is a quote from Nicole saying she wishes her stepdad and stepsister would go away and her father would return. But her story isn't that simple, because she likes her stepbrother, Connor, and doesn't want him to go away.

"Connor is on my side most of the time. He sticks up for me," she says.

In most stepfamilies, kids gain something special, something they never thought they'd have. For Nicole, she's gained a stepbrother who plays with her and supports her, even when his dad is mad at her.

Take a minute to look at your new stepfamily. It may not be what you asked for or wanted, but it's yours. Try to find some of the good in it, if possible. It could be the half-hour every Friday your stepdad shoots hoops with you. Or maybe you like the fact that now you have several adults attending all your dance recitals or track meets.

Stepkids Speak Out

My stepdad is fun and he's nice to me. He treats me like his real daughter.
—LINDSAY

In my stepfamily, I have two completely different lives, and a second home to escape to. I'm not stuck in one place. —OLIVIA

My stepsister and I do sports and lots of fun things together. —PAIGE

It's fun when my mom invites my stepcousin—on my dad's side—to come swimming with my mom and me. Then both sides of my family are together.
—ANTHONY

What's Good About Your Stepfamily?

Grab a pen and your Survival Log. On the left side of a page, list some things you like about your stepfamily. On the right side, list some ways you can make these things even more enjoyable.

Your page might look something like this:

Four Things I Like About My Stepfamily	How to Make These Things Even Better
1. I like being with my stepsister.	**1.** I could ask to see my stepsister more often, even when she's at her other parent's home.
2. I like being a big sis to my baby stepbrother.	**2.** I could ask my stepmom if I can help take care of the baby more often.
3. My friends think my stepdad is cool. He's nice and he's really different from their dads.	**3.** I could invite my stepdad to play basketball with my friends and me.
4. I now have another adult— my stepmom—to go to if I need to talk.	**4.** Next time I'm upset, I'll ask for my stepmom's advice.

Imagine You're a Student in a Foreign Land

Let's try another activity. Imagine you're a foreign exchange student. That's a school kid who goes to live in another country with a new family for a few months or a whole school year. Pretend you're traveling to Germany, to live for a year in the home of two new adults and two new kids. What an adventure! You're about to move in with a family you've never met before.

How would you deal with this situation? List your answers to the following questions in your Survival Log.

1. How would you try to get to know this family?

2. What kinds of interests would you want to share with them?

3. What things would you want them to know about you?

Might you use these same ideas to get to know the people in your new stepfamily? Think of your stepfamily situation as an adventure, too—but without expensive plane tickets or long airport lines!

Step-Tween Survival Tips

I know it might feel weird at first to have new family members, like stepgrandparents. If all they want to do is love and care for you, let them. It may take a while, but you'll hopefully learn to enjoy them. —*PILAR*

At first, I felt like I didn't have anything in common with my stepbrother. He's two years younger and I felt we were two completely different people. When he hit fifth grade, that's when we started having the same interests. —*JAKE*

Reality Check:
What If You Just Don't Get Along
with Everyone?

You may find that being patient, expressing your feelings, keeping a sense of humor, and thinking positively still don't help you feel comfortable around your new stepfamily. Maybe one of the adults or kids in your home is mean to you or treats you badly. Or maybe one or more of your stepsiblings is bullying you, causing you to feel unsafe or like they're "ganging up" on you. If any of this is happening, tell someone. Seek out a parent, teacher, or school counselor. You might begin by saying something like, "I'm having some problems with how a family member is treating me. Can I talk to you about it?" As a last resort, you may ask to spend less time at one parent's home.

Stepping Closer

Are you confused about what an isosceles triangle is? Are you unsure about the difference between an attributive and a demonstrative adjective? You might discover new people in your life now to help you make sense of the stuff you're learning in school. Ask around. There might be a math whiz or wordsmith in your stepfamily who would be very happy to help you.

CHAPTER 5

How to Make Your New Home Feel More Like *Home*

Stepkids Speak Out

In our house, I had to share a bedroom with my stepsister. It was hard sharing the kitchen and all the other rooms with my new stepfamily. Sometimes I felt as if I had nowhere private to go. —CHLOE

After my parents got divorced and remarried, I had to give up all my pets. I moved to a new city and lost all my friendships. I moved in with my dad and stepmom, and my stepmom was too busy with a new baby to deal with me. —JONATHAN

Like Jonathan and Chloe, you've probably been through some big changes in your day-to-day life. Your new stepparent and stepsiblings may have moved in with you and your parent. Or perhaps you moved out of your old place, and you're now sharing a bedroom with a stepsister who listens to country music while you prefer hip-hop. Or maybe you just feel a little weird hanging out in your bathrobe with your stepmom around.

How can you feel at home when you're now living under the same roof with total strangers? How can you be comfortable when you're at your dad's place only one day a week, and now he's got a new baby?

In this chapter, you'll get some tips for learning how to share your living space while creating your very own "nest" that looks and feels right to you. You'll hear how Chloe, Jonathan, and other stepkids learned to deal with their new living arrangements and even feel happy and comfortable.

Eight Ways to Make Your New Place Feel More Like Home

Since your parents' divorce, you probably spend at least some time at a different home. It makes sense to try to make yourself comfortable there. Here are some ideas for doing that:

1. Put away that suitcase

Rather than living out of a suitcase, unpack your things. Make sure you've got enough clothes, books, and essentials (like a toothbrush and shampoo) at both your parents' homes. You can divide up the clothes you have, and maybe ask for a few extra pairs of socks and jeans.

2. Show your style

If it's okay with your parents and stepparents, grab a paintbrush and paint the walls of your new bedroom with your favorite color. Make a floor plan for your room, showing where you want your bed, dresser, and other furniture to be. If you're sharing a room, ask your stepsibling or sibling to join you in this project. Working together like this, you'll probably learn a lot about each other.

3. Hold onto your memories

Once you've decorated your new room, you might decide to keep that Winnie the Pooh lamp you got for your fifth birthday or that worn old bedspread with the soft fabric. These things may bring back happy memories. They may give you comfort. Whatever the reason, feel free to hold onto some of the things that give you that "homey" feeling.

4. Keep in touch with friends

Whether your "second home" is around the corner or 1,000 miles away, you can still stay close to your friends. Send them emails, photos, IMs, or handwritten letters. Make regular phone calls, too, and try to plan visits. Staying connected with old friends can help you feel connected wherever you are. And if you're still in the same town, be sure to invite your friends over. Ask your parents and stepparents if you can have a sleepover or an art party or simply invite a friend over for the afternoon.

5. Treat your taste buds

You might not want to quench your thirst with your stepsister's Supergreen Smoothies made from seaweed and zucchini. Ask your parent or stepparent to keep the refrigerator and cupboards stocked with some of your favorite juices, sandwich ingredients, snacks, or desserts. That way, when you're hungry in your new home, familiar and tasty food is available.

6. Explore your new neighborhood

Do some research online or at the library to learn about your new surroundings. With the help of your parent and stepparent, get out and explore! Find those parks, pools, and community centers where kids your age hang out. Locate the best cafes and clothing stores. Scout for bike trails and beaches. Getting familiar with your neighborhood and the people in it is key to feeling at home.

7. Spend time with your new roommate

If you suddenly find yourself sharing a room with a sibling or stepsibling— don't fight it. Try to get to know your new roomie better. It's a big change going from having your own room to sharing a room. But it can have its pluses. You might find you share the same taste in music, books, or video games, the same taste in decorating, or even the same taste and size in clothes. Better yet, your roommate might introduce you to new music, books, games, or clothes that you'll really love. Remember, this is all new to both of you. It could be fun to experience these changes together.

8. Think about what you need to feel at home

While you're taking time to set up your space and explore your neighborhood, think about what makes you feel "at home," and ask for it. Be realistic about what's possible. Asking for an Olympic-size swimming pool might not go over too well!

Think about which of the following things apply to you, and then list some of your own ideas in your Survival Log.

What I Need to Feel "at Home"

* A parent who's willing to listen when I'm upset and give me a hug when I'm feeling sad.

* A parent or sibling who will spend time playing games or doing activities with me.

* My pet, and a place for it to sleep and play.

* My favorite quilt, pillow, or stuffed animal.

* A phone I can use to talk with my friends.

* A desk where I can do my homework without interruptions.

* My own area of a shared bedroom (or my own room) that I can decorate how I want.

* A computer with an Internet connection.

* Art supplies and a place where I can be creative (and sometimes make a little mess!).

* A place where I can practice my musical instrument without bothering others.

* My favorite books and a reading lamp.

* An outdoor space or a nearby park where I can play ball, plant a garden, or just sit and relax in the sun.

Survival Tool #7:
Ask for What You Need

Now that you've made a list of what you need to feel at home, pick five that are most important to you and that seem the most doable.

Using I-messages and Straight Talk, get together with your parent (and your stepparent, if you want). Describe what you'd like to have. You might begin by saying something like, "This book I'm reading suggested that I figure out what I need to feel at home in my stepfamily. I thought long and hard about it. I'd really appreciate it if you would help me paint my room and find a place where I can play with my dog."

Survival Tool #8:
Brainstorm

Brainstorming is all about coming up with creative new ideas. People often brainstorm in groups to solve a problem. You can also do it alone. The key is to accept *all* ideas that come up, no matter how whacky they seem at first. Then, narrow the list of ideas using logic and common sense.

For example, let's say your parents and stepparents can't grant all five wishes. Instead of throwing a tantrum or sulking, brainstorm other ideas that might work for everyone. Use your imagination and be flexible. If some of your wishes aren't doable, come up with new ways of meeting your needs.

If they say, "There's no room here to throw a ball with Scooby," you might say, "Can you take me to the park down the street?" If they say, "We don't have the time to repaint your room right now," you might say, "I'd like to do the painting myself, and maybe ask my friends to help."

Brainstorming ideas is important to thriving in a stepfamily. In fact, it's a valuable skill to use in every part of your life. Your experience as part of a stepfamily will likely help you learn life skills like brainstorming much faster than you would otherwise!

Step-Tween Survival Tip

When I had to share a room with a stepsister who loved puppy dog posters, I decided to live with it. We each had our own side of the room. I decided to focus on what I could control. I decorated my side with my art nouveau posters. I had a canopy bed that created an island of space for me. I also reminded myself that my stepsister had to look at my posters, and probably didn't like them. —*CHLOE*

Sharing Your Space

Sharing your living space often requires brainstorming new solutions. Let's take a look at how you might deal with some stepfamily space-sharing dilemmas.

Know Yourself: What Do You Do When You Need Some Peace and Quiet?

Say you like to study in a quiet place, but your stepsister plays loud music in your shared bedroom every afternoon.

Choose the answer that best describes how you would behave in this situation.

> a) I quit studying and tell my teachers that my poor grades are my stepsister's fault.
>
> b) I blast music even louder on my side of the room to make a point (and probably make her mad).
>
> c) I calmly let my stepsister know I'm being tested on a really hard grammar chapter tomorrow and I'd like her to turn down her music or wear headphones, at least until I've finished studying.

Answer "a" is clearly not in your best interests. There's not a teacher in the world who will buy your "My stepsister plays her music too loud" excuse. So forget that idea. This may be a tough situation for you right now, but it's important to stay focused on solutions, not excuses.

Answer "b" is just going to get you in a stickier situation with your stepsister, and it'll likely give you a headache, too. That's probably not the personal space solution you're looking for.

The "c" response is your best bet, and here's why: There's a good chance your stepsister isn't blasting her music to annoy you. Maybe she simply likes it loud. Give her the benefit of the doubt—in other words, assume she doesn't realize you can't study with electric guitar blaring in your ears. Take the opportunity to respectfully tell her what you need. Approach her with Straight Talk and a good attitude, and maybe even appeal to her sense of pity (she might not like studying grammar, either). She just might agree to use headphones or turn down the volume.

Of course there's always a chance that even your Straight Talk won't work. Your next step may be to talk with your parent or stepparent. You could also try to find a quieter spot in your home to study until you work out a better solution. In the meantime, remember this: It's not always easy to share space with a sibling or stepsibling. But it can be done. Get together to brainstorm ideas that might work for both of you. What does each of you need to feel happy and comfortable in your shared room?

 ## Stepkids Speak Out

When we all moved into our house, there wasn't enough room for everyone to have a bedroom. So my mom and stepdad gave me the playroom as a bedroom. They said I got to have the biggest bedroom, as long as I shared it as a playroom with my stepsiblings. At first, this seemed like a good thing. But whenever my stepbrother and stepsister came over, just after I got home from school, they'd rush upstairs and invade my room, which didn't even have a door on it.
—ANTHONY

Know Yourself: What Do You Do When You Need a Little Privacy?

Choose the answer that best describes how you would behave in this situation.

If you were Anthony, what would you do?

a) Tell them you don't like your space invaded right after school. Ask them if they have any ideas about how to change the situation.

b) Play with them in your room even though you don't want to, or else quietly leave every time they come in.

c) Tell your stepsiblings, "It's my room, and I don't want to share it anymore. I never should have agreed to this."

If you chose "a," you might have a future career as a world leader! Telling your stepsiblings how you feel, and then asking for their help to find possible solutions can be a very effective way to resolve a dilemma.

If you chose "b," you're still stuck in a tough situation. This response will probably just make you feel angry and resentful of your stepsiblings. Ask yourself, "Is this really the solution I'm looking for?"

If you chose "c," you're not likely to get any closer to a solution. Your stepsiblings and parents may think you're being unreasonable. After all, you got the biggest room because you agreed to share it as a playroom.

How Anthony's Family Solved This Problem

In this case, Anthony talked to his mom, who asked everyone to sit down together for a "Brainstorming Session." In other words, they agreed to think of a bunch of possible solutions to find one that might work for the whole family.

Here's how this kind of session might go:

Anthony: "Hi guys. Thanks for getting together to help me solve this problem. Here's the deal: I'm okay sharing my room as a playroom most of the time. But I also need some time to myself to just chill out."

Louis (Anthony's stepbrother): "I know what you mean. It's just that we like hanging out in the playroom, too. That's where we watch TV and play games."

Claire (Anthony's stepsister): "Yeah, and we want to watch shows and play games *with* you, Anthony. It's not like we're trying to take over your room!"

Steve (Anthony's stepdad): "Well, let's look at the situation. Anthony agreed to share his bedroom so everyone can have a playroom. Claire and Louis, you like having extra space to play. You also like spending time with Anthony. What ideas do you have about how we can handle this?"

Diana (Anthony's mom): "Let's brainstorm. First, one of us shares an idea, and then the next person, and so on. Don't say whether you think it's a good idea or not. Just let everyone have a turn. Then we can talk about the ideas."

Claire: "Okay, I'll go first. How about if Anthony has his private time at night? That way, I get to see him right after school and hang out, and he'll still have time later to listen to music and stuff."

Louis: "Or maybe we should move some of our games out of Anthony's room so we don't always need to go there to play."

Steve: "Or we could post some type of sign-up sheet to let Anthony know when others want to use his room as the playroom."

Diana: "Any thoughts on these ideas?"

Anthony: "I'm not sure if the sign-up sheet would work because people still might sign up for too much time before I get a chance to sign up for mine..."

Diana: "Good point, Anthony. And Louis, it sounded like a good idea to move things out of Anthony's room, but our space is pretty limited and I don't think I'd want everyone's things all over the living room or crowding the bedrooms."

Claire: "What about my idea? Anthony could have his private time later."

Anthony: "Claire, I like hanging out with you and Louis and I'm always happy to see you. But I also like relaxing by myself right after school. It would be hard to wait all night for some time alone."

Diana: "Maybe that's it. I wonder if everyone could agree to give Anthony a little time after school—maybe an hour—before he turns his bedroom into the playroom. That way, he'll have his bedroom to himself, but he'll also have plenty of time to spend with Claire and Louis."

Anthony: "That might work. An hour would be enough."

Steve: "Okay. We'll give Anthony an hour after school to use his room alone. Then we can open it up as the playroom. Let's try this for one week and then we can meet again on Sunday and figure out how it's working."

Four Ways to Deal When Your Space Is Invaded

1. Live with it

Like Chloe (who had to live with the puppy dog posters), you may realize that sharing space is just as hard for your stepsibling as it is for you. You may decide it's not really so bad camping out with this new person, even though you don't like her way of decorating. Try to make the best of this situation. Fix up your side of the room. Get to know other things about your stepsiblings, besides just their taste in bedroom art. You might end up staying up until midnight telling each other ghost stories or looking at comic books together.

2. Talk to your stepsiblings

Like Anthony, you may decide to talk to your stepsiblings. They might be surprised at how you feel, and you might be surprised at how they feel. Try to work out a solution. If you're sharing a room, you may decide that one of you has the room after school until dinnertime, and the other one gets it after dinner until bedtime. Or, like Anthony, you may decide it's more fun to be in your room together, as long as each of you gets just a little time alone.

3. Talk to your parent or stepparent

If you don't feel comfortable talking to your stepsiblings right away, ask your stepparent or parent for help. Together, you may be able to think of possible solutions. Then you could meet with your stepsiblings (alone or with your parent and stepparent) and share your ideas. Be sure to give your stepsiblings time to share their ideas, too!

4. Participate in a family meeting

Your parent or stepparent might want to invite all family members to meet together, like Anthony's family did. In family meetings, everyone gets to talk and everyone is expected to listen. Hopefully, the group can think of an idea or two worth trying.

While you're at it, don't forget to laugh when you can. Even though living with new family members can be challenging, there can be plenty of funny moments and good times, too.

 **Step-Tween Survival Tip**

Even though I was suddenly living with all these people and felt like I never had any privacy, I found ways to laugh. We all had a friendly competition over who could make people laugh. You need to come up with jokes you can share together. —CHLOE

Reality Check:
When It Feels Like Nobody's Listening

You may find that brainstorming is not working for you. In this case, it's important to ask for help. Find an adult who will listen to you. You might say to your parent or a counselor, "I didn't feel very good about how the brainstorming in our family meeting went. I felt like nobody listened to my ideas." Your parent or counselor may be able to help you practice communicating your ideas in a group so that people will be more likely to listen. He or she may also be able to help you express how it feels when people don't listen to you.

Stepping Closer

Get to know your stepsibling better by throwing a pizza and movie party. Order a pizza and watch a movie together. Afterwards share what you liked and didn't like about the movie. Talk about other movies you both have seen and what you thought of them.

CHAPTER 6

When Mom's Place and Dad's Place Are Really Different

 ## Stepkids Speak Out

My stepdad acts like a father figure without trying to make me feel like he's my father. He's brought authority to our house that we needed. But at my dad's house, it's different. My dad doesn't have rules. There's not much authority there. —JAKE

After my parents remarried, it felt like I had multiple identities. At my mom's house, my mom was a vegetarian and didn't have a TV. My stepdad came from an old-fashioned farm family. All of a sudden, we were going to church with him. At my dad's house, before my stepmom came along, there weren't any rules. —ANNA

At my mom's house, my stepdad is a really good stepdad. He took me in like I was his own son. Whenever he buys his kids something, he buys me something. And when he takes his kids somewhere, to a ballgame, or the mall, he takes me, too. At my dad's and stepmom's, it's different. I don't go there a lot. —ZIAD

Stories like Jake's, Anna's, and Ziad's are common. One parent's home might have few rules and you're allowed to sail through the kitchen wearing in-line skates. You may also get to stay up past midnight guzzling soda and eating candy. While your other parent's place might have a lot more rules, and things like soda and candy are strictly off-limits.

Says Lindsay, "We have different rules at different houses. My mom and my dad are very different, way different."

You'll find tips here for dealing with the differences at your two homes (if you're one of the step-tweens who lives in two homes). You'll get advice from kids who've been there.

Like many stepkids, you are probably willing to accept some differences. Because you want to spend time with both of your parents, you might be fine with the fact that your mom lets you stay up until midnight, while your dad insists on an early bedtime.

It's okay if you feel like one place is more like your home than the other. That's probably the place where you spend more time, keep more of your things, and have more friends nearby. And maybe you are okay with it. But maybe sometimes you feel confused and even a little upset about favoring one of your parent's places over the other.

You may want both places to feel more similar. You might wish that your stepdad would make the same ham-and-cheese omelet that your dad makes. Or that your dad's place had the same cozy couch as your mom's. Just as important, you may want a stepparent or stepsibling to be more welcoming of you. If any of these kinds of things are making you uncomfortable, you've got a number of choices.

Five Things to Do When You Prefer One Place Over the Other

1. Accept it

Like Jake, you might decide that there's not much you can do to change your situation. You might accept it and make the best of it. Jake likes to keep things light and laugh at what happens at his dad's house. He says that it's fun going to a home where there aren't many rules about TV time or what he should eat for breakfast.

2. Make some changes

If you'd like to make one of your two homes feel more comfortable, review the **Eight Ways to Make Your New Place Feel More Like Home** on pages 45–47. Add some favorite posters or quilts in your bedroom. Ask for help stocking the refrigerator with your favorite foods. Get to know your neighbors. Then have a chat with your mom or dad about what they could do, along with your stepparents, to make you feel more at ease.

3. Talk it out

Talk to your mom, dad, stepparents, another trusted adult, or a counselor about how you feel. Maybe you feel guilty that you prefer your mom's place over your dad's. Talking about this can help you feel better and more comfortable.

4. Note the pluses

Find things you do like at your "other" home. Even though you're not crazy about your stepdad, you might really like your stepbrother. Your stepmom may have taught you how to cook Russian food or play a new card game. And maybe your stepsister shares her music downloads, books, and magazines with you. It can be helpful to notice the good things.

5. Find what's funny

If you travel between two homes across town, you might playfully call your mom's place your "western headquarters" and your dad's place your "eastern headquarters." Or maybe your stepdad cooks only healthy food, prompting you to say something like, "Mmm...I can feel those B vitamins making me healthier and more stress-free right this moment, thanks to this squash!" Sometimes humor like this can help you handle difficult situations. Give it a try if you're comfortable with it.

 Step-Tween Survival Tip

It's important to have a sense of humor. We called ourselves "The Branson Bunch," a twisted version of the 1970s TV show, *The Brady Bunch.* —CHLOE

Be Flexible

You might prefer your dad's cooking to your stepdad's. Maybe you wish you got to eat the same food at both your homes. That's okay, but it may not be possible. Instead, think of ways you could be flexible. Brainstorm some possible solutions.

Make a list of all the things you could do to feel better about meals at your mom and stepdad's place. Here are some ideas to get you started:

When You Don't Like Your Stepdad's Cooking Because It's Not Like Your Dad's

✳ Ask for an extra helping of a side dish if you don't like the main dish.

✳ Search online or find a cookbook and pick out some recipes you like. Offer to help cook.

✳ Every once in a while, try your stepdad's tuna-and-peas casserole. You may just end up liking it!

✳ Ask your stepdad if you can go to the grocery store with him, and tell him which foods you like best.

✳ Announce that you'll only eat chocolate cake with candy sprinkles for dinner. (Just kidding.)

Know Yourself: What Do You Do When You Need Some Peace and Quiet?

Answer the following question to see how far you're ready to "flex" with your stepfamily.

Let's say at your dad's place, there's just you, your sister, your dad, and your stepmom. It's quiet, and the only visitors are your friends and your sister's friends.

Meanwhile, at your mom's, you live with your two stepbrothers, your stepdad, and your stepbrothers' 29-year-old cousin (your stepcousin), who was supposed to move into his own place six months ago. Every time you go over to your mom's, your stepbrothers, your stepcousin, and four or so of their friends are throwing around basketballs, blaring music, and making a mess in the kitchen.

What would you do in this situation?

a) Hide in your bedroom (assuming you're the only one in it!) and wish you were back at your dad's place.

b) Consider how you might be able to tolerate these people and the commotion, at least for short periods of time.

c) Scream at your stepbrothers, stepcousin, and their friends, "You're loud and obnoxious, you make terrible food, and you invade my space!"

If you chose "a," you're not ready to "flex." You'd rather be in a place that feels comfortable and familiar. That's a common feeling, especially when you're in a new situation. The good news is that you know how you feel and you're not taking your feelings out on everyone around you. Just try not to hold your feelings inside. Hiding might feel good for a little while, but it's important to find an outlet for your feelings. Take another look at Chapter 1 for some ideas about how to let those feelings out.

If you chose "b," you must be in an adventurous and flexible mood. Chances are, you regularly look for ways to "go with the flow" and cope with all kinds of situations.

If you chose "c," you're likely angry about feeling so invaded. You have strong feelings and want to get them out in the open right now. It's good that you want to express yourself and let others know when you're feeling upset. But if you scream first and think about the consequences later, you aren't using your best Straight Talk. What's more, you probably won't be any closer to finding a way to cope with the situation at your mom's place.

Five Ways to Enjoy Your Mom's Place, Even When It's Really Different From Your Dad's

1. Accept that your parents' places are different. Instead of trying to make them identical, see how it feels to be okay with their differences. You might try to find the humor in all the commotion. When you're at your dad's, maybe you'll enjoy the peace and quiet that much more.

2. Ask your stepbrothers, stepcousin, and their friends to teach you how to dribble a basketball or do another activity they're good at.

3. Introduce your stepbrothers to some of the music you like, and ask if they'd be interested in listening to it once in a while.

4. Ask your mom (or your stepdad) for a little one-on-one time while the others are playing basketball and doing their thing.

5. Ask permission to invite one of your friends over so you don't feel so outnumbered. Find a quiet place where you two can do something you enjoy.

Add some ideas of your own in your Survival Log.

When Your Parent Doesn't Want You to Enjoy Your New Family

Maybe you're thinking, "What if I am enjoying myself at one of my parent's homes, but my other parent doesn't want me to?" Sometimes, parents have a hard time adjusting to change, too. For instance, your dad might still be angry over the divorce, and he may not like it when you spend time with his ex-wife (your mom) and her new husband (your stepdad) at their home. He may be jealous of your stepdad and stepsiblings, especially if you seem to be enjoying your time with them. He might even be afraid that you'll like your new stepdad more than him, or that your stepdad will try to replace him as your real dad.

All of these feelings are common among divorced parents, and none of them are your fault. But they can certainly create some prickly situations for you.

Take another example: Let's say your mom is really upset that your dad is remarried. She doesn't want you to enjoy your stepmom or have any fun at your dad's place. What do you do?

Step-Tween Survival Tip

If one of your parents tries to turn you against your new stepparent, listen to both sides of the story before you make any judgment. Once you hear both sides, it might change your opinion. Don't jump to any conclusions. —TAYLOR

Straight Talk with Parents Who Don't Seem to Want You to Enjoy Your "Other" Home

Here's where you pull out your best Straight Talk and I-messages, and try this special three-step process:

	Situation A	Situation B	Situation C
	Your mom tries to get you to stay at her place instead of going to your dad's.	Your mom says mean things about your stepmom.	Your dad seems jealous of your stepdad. At your basketball games, your dad sits all by himself and gives your stepdad mean looks when he cheers for you.
Step 1	Recognize that she's having a hard time adjusting to the changes.	Again, recognize that she's having a hard time.	Show that you understand he is having a hard time.
Example	"Mom, I know it's hard for you when I go to Dad's place."	"Mom, I know you don't like that Dad is remarried."	"Dad, I know it's hard for you that mom is married, and that I live with them part of the time."
Step 2	Explain how you feel about her.	Explain how you feel about her.	Explain how you feel about him.
Example	"I love you no matter what, and I like being with you."	"I like my stepmom and her kids, but I still love you as much as ever."	"Even though I like my stepdad, he'll never replace you as my dad."
Step 3	Tell her how you feel and what you want.	Tell her how you feel and what you want.	Tell him how you feel and what you want.
Example	"But I want to see Dad, too. And I have fun with my stepbrother. I wish you wouldn't try to get me to stay with you all of the time."	"It upsets me when you say mean things about my stepmom in front of me. I wish you'd stop."	"It makes me uncomfortable that you seem so upset at my games when my stepdad cheers for me. Could you go easier on him? I like having lots of cheerleaders!"

Talking about difficult issues like these is not easy. But if you feel comfortable, give it a try! If you're not ready to express yourself directly to your parent or stepparent, talk to an adult you trust.

Reality Check: When My Parent Is Still Making It Hard for Me to Enjoy My New Family

If Straight Talk doesn't work and your parent's behavior is still upsetting you, talk to your other parent. Talk to a counselor, at school or elsewhere. You might even ask the parent who's upsetting you to visit a counselor with you. You might say, "I really want to talk to you about how you feel about my life at my other home. Maybe we could go to a counselor together."

Stepping Closer

Playing sports or games can be a great way to feel closer to people you don't know well. You don't necessarily have to talk a lot, but you're doing something fun together. Ask your stepparent and stepsibling to throw a ball or play a board game. Be sure to mix up the sides. Offer to be your stepdad's or stepbrother's partner. Focus on working together—not on winning!

CHAPTER 7

What to Do When You Have a New Bedtime (or Other Rule), But Not the One You Want

It's natural to want things, but demanding to have something isn't very realistic or polite. Whether you're living in a stepfamily, hanging out with friends at the mall, or playing on a sports team, it's important to know how to ask for what you want.

In this chapter, you'll learn another survival tool: compromising and negotiating. Along with Straight Talk and I-messages, it's all about communicating with others in a way that helps you—and the people you're talking to—get what you want and need.

compromise: (verb) to find a middle way between two extremes

negotiate: (verb) to bargain or discuss a subject in order to agree

Survival Tool #9:
Compromise and Negotiate

Compromising involves finding a solution that brings you to the middle ground between different points of view. For example, if your stepdad wants you to keep your room neater, but you're not a neat-freak, suggest that you pick up your room on special occasions— when guests will be at your home, for example.

Negotiating is what you do to reach a compromise. It's what happens when two or more people try to find a solution they're all comfortable with. In the room-cleaning case, you negotiate when you ask your stepdad if you can clean your room on special occasions. You might also explain why you think it's a good idea. And your stepdad gets to present his side of the argument and explain why he thinks you should clean more often.

If you don't convince your stepdad to budge on cleanliness during your negotiations, your next compromise might be to clean your room once a week instead—which is more often than when guests visit, but less often than every day.

Otherwise Known as "C & N"

"Compromise" and "negotiate" are long words that often appear in school spelling bees. To keep things simple, let's refer to them as "C & N."

So to review, C & N involves:

* Letting someone know your wants and needs

* Listening to the other person's point of view

* Working toward an agreement that feels okay for everyone involved

 Step-Tween Survival Tips

Whining and crying doesn't get you what you want. Sometimes one parent will buy it, but the other parent won't and you'll get in trouble. —*ETHAN*

Sometimes if you make a sacrifice for everyone else, someone else will make a sacrifice for your sake. If I have to be with the whole family one time, the next time, my dad will do something just with me. —*JAKE*

Three Things to Remember About C & N

1. They're not sure things

Compromising and negotiating can make it easier to ask for—and get—what you want, but they won't work all the time. Simply asking for something using C & N doesn't mean you'll get it. Think of compromising and negotiating as tools in your survival backpack. They're not the only gear in your pack, but they may be just the things you need when you're trying to get through a difficult situation.

2. You can only control how *you* communicate

Keep in mind that you can't control how other people express themselves, only how you do. Even if you try out your best C & N skills on your parents, stepparents, siblings, or stepsiblings, they may not practice theirs! But you can stick with yours, and maybe even teach your friends and family a thing or two.

3. Be patient

Like Straight Talk, C & N skills don't develop overnight. It takes time to become a good compromiser and negotiator. Keep trying and hang in there!

When to Use C & N

Compromising and negotiating can come in handy in many different circumstances.

When Your Stepmom Says You Can't Stay Up Late Anymore

Before my dad married my stepmom, I stayed up as late as I wanted. Then Carmen entered the situation and tried to tell me I couldn't stay up late anymore. —ANNA

In this case, how could Anna negotiate and compromise with her stepmom? Here's a sample conversation:

Anna: "I understand you're trying to look after me, and I appreciate that. Here's my problem, though. I'm used to staying up as late as I want at my dad's. It feels strange having you tell me what to do here."

At this point, Anna might try to negotiate with Carmen by suggesting some other choices.

Carmen: "I don't think it's healthy for you to stay up so late all the time. You seem so tired. I think you'd feel better if you got more sleep."

Anna: "Can we find a compromise? Let's say I go to bed at 9 on weeknights, but on Saturday nights, I get to stay up until 11. Or maybe I could stay up later on weeknights—like, until 9:30—if I get all my chores done early in the week.

Carmen: "How about you move that Saturday night bedtime to 10:30, and stick with 9 on weeknights? That seems reasonable to me."

Anna: "Okay, I'm willing to give it a try. But every once in a while I'd like to stay up later, like when I have a friend over and we're watching a movie."

Carmen: "Let's see how it goes, and keep talking."

Notice how Anna and Carmen worked together to find a compromise they both could live with, while leaving room to negotiate more later, if needed. C & N is sometimes not a quick one-time fix. Several rounds of negotiations may be required to reach a lasting solution.

Step-Tween Survival Tip

If your parents or stepparents want you to do one thing, and you want to do something different, give them some choices. Give them a choice of three or four things you want to do. Kids need to tell parents what they want to do and give them options. Then ask them to decide on one. This way, the kid is flexible, too. —*ETHAN*

When Your Stepbrother Talks Loudly on His Phone in Your Room

You really like your privacy and you enjoy having a quiet space to read, study, and draw. You share a room with your stepbrother, Jesse, who constantly chats with friends on his cell phone in a loud voice.

You may have already tried some of the survival tools from previous chapters, such as Straight Talk, to let Jesse know that you'd really appreciate it if he could keep his voice down while you're at your desk. You might have even decided to spend more time with your stepbrother, thinking that his talking wouldn't bother you as much once you got used to it. But none of these ideas seemed to do the trick.

It may be time to try the twin tools of compromising and negotiating. In a stepfamily, you need them just as much as you need batteries, flashlights, and water on a camping trip.

Write the Lines to Your Own Stepfamily Survival Script

You know the storyline. Here's the cast of characters so you can keep them straight:

You are the stepkid who isn't used to sharing your space. You're looking for quiet time and learning new skills for asking for what you want.

Jesse is your loud, chatty stepbrother who probably means well and isn't used to sharing space, either.

. . . .

You: "Hey, Jesse. I know we've talked about figuring out a way to share our room while you talk to your friends and I try to read. But it hasn't been working out that well. You still want a place to talk with your friends and I still like having a quiet room. I understand how you feel. I just wonder if we can work something out so we can both get what we want."

Jesse: "Huh? Wait a minute—I have to make a call…"

You: "Maybe we can…(insert your idea for a compromise here)."

Brainstorm some ideas and write them in your Survival Log. Here are a few compromises you might suggest to Jesse:

You: "Maybe we can agree to a list of days and times when the room can be used for 'alone time.' That way, we can plan ahead and know when the room will be all our own. You'll get it so you can talk on the phone. I'll get it so I can have some quiet time to study."

You: "Maybe you wouldn't mind texting or emailing your friends instead of talking on the phone while I'm studying. Would that be okay with you?"

You: "I could probably do my sketches or other stuff while you're talking, but if I have to study, would you agree to go somewhere else to talk?"

When Your Stepdad Forbids Computer Games

Let's say you go to your mom's place every other weekend, and you like to play a game on the computer from time to time. Your stepdad doesn't approve of electronic game playing, because he thinks it's a bad influence on your younger stepsister, Sasha.

Begin by using your best Straight Talk. Tell your stepdad you don't want to harm your little sister in any way. But you'd like to play a computer game every once in a while. Then, follow with compromising and negotiating to find a solution.

Here's a sample script of how this might look:

You: "I know you're worried how it will affect Sasha if I play computer games at home."

Stepdad: "You're right. I don't approve of them."

You: "But what if I find a way to play my game every once in a while when Sasha isn't around to watch? And what if I limited my time playing it?"

Stepdad: "Hmmm. That's an interesting idea. Keep talking."

You: "How about I only play my game during the two hours on Saturday when Sasha's at her dance class. And if there's no class, I don't play it."

Stepdad: "So, you'd only play it for a couple of hours when she's not here?"

You: "Yeah. That way, she doesn't see it, but I still get time to play it."

Stepdad: "This might work. Let me think about it."

Stepkids Speak Out

My older stepsister takes my clothes. I have gone to both my stepmom and dad asking them for help. She doesn't stop. There is nothing else my parents can do. I need to negotiate with her. —TAYLOR

When Your Stepsister Borrows Your Clothes Without Asking

If you were in Taylor's position, what would you do? Here are some things you might suggest:

You: "How about you wear one of my outfits once a week, but only after you've asked me first?"

You: "Let's go through my clothes and decide what I'm willing to give up. Maybe there's something I don't need."

You: "I really like your silver-and-jade earrings. How about you trade me the earrings for my jean skirt?"

You: "How about I borrow your silver-and-jade earrings once a week, and you get to borrow my jean skirt that day?"

Add your own ideas in your Survival Log.

What if even after you offer compromises, your chatty stepbrother or your clothes-borrowing stepsister isn't interested in your suggestions? You could a) rack your brain thinking of 100 more ideas, hoping one of them will work; b) sleep with your dog on the living room couch to avoid your stepsibling; or c) try to negotiate a compromise with him or her.

Always keep in mind that the best compromises come from negotiating together.

Things to Avoid When You're Compromising and Negotiating

Don't treat compromising and negotiating like a competition. The goal isn't to have a winner and a loser. Instead, the goal is to work out a solution that everyone can live with. That may mean changing your original request.

Don't lose your cool. It's easy to get worked up when you're asking for something you want. However, it's also easy to lose someone's willingness to listen, and even to get in trouble and lose privileges when you start yelling, blaming, or name-calling. Remember your **Six Tips for Using Straight Talk** on pages 19–22. Try to stay calm when you communicate and use I-messages.

Don't confuse compromising with giving up. Compromising involves agreeing to something that may not have been your first choice, but that you're still comfortable with. Compromising is not about giving up and giving in. It's not about ignoring your own needs. Don't strike a compromise that doesn't feel right to you. Don't bury your feelings away instead of expressing them. If you find yourself giving up after trying to compromise, talk about it with an adult you trust.

Things to Remember When You're Compromising and Negotiating

Do be clear and respectful about what you want. State your request clearly and respectfully. Say something like, "Dad, I know you'd like me to spend most of my time with you when I'm here, but I also want to spend some time with my friends on the weekend. Can we talk about this?"

Do keep an open mind. Be open to different solutions. Can you be flexible with your bedtime? Are you willing to rearrange some of your time with friends? Think about when you might bend a little.

Do listen to the other side. Before you start rattling off the 10 reasons you should be able to eat Sugar Shockers for breakfast, take time to see the other point of view. Be willing to look through the eyes of the people you're negotiating with. Try to understand why they feel the way they do. This will make it a lot easier to find a solution everyone can feel good about.

Reality Check:
When C & N Isn't Enough

Compromising and negotiating are great survival tools, but they aren't appropriate for every situation. If you're in a situation that's uncomfortable, unsafe, or upsetting, don't try to handle it on your own. For example, let's say that your stepsister is actually stealing your clothes, or that your stepbrother is viewing "adult" Internet sites in your room. In these cases, you need to tell someone—preferably your parent or stepparent—so he or she can intervene. Some behaviors are simply not open to compromise or negotiation.

Stepping Closer

Have you had a hard day of negotiations? Do you feel like you need a laugh? Chances are your stepsiblings do, too. Invite them to play a silly board game with you, or play "Charades." Laughing together can often make things seem more bearable.

CHAPTER 8

When Your Stepsibling Gets to Watch TV and You Don't: What's Fair?

 ## Stepkids Speak Out

It seemed unfair to me that my mom didn't let me watch TV at all, and my stepbrothers and stepsister got to watch it whenever the wanted. My mom thought they watched way too much TV, and her way of dealing with it was not letting me watch any at all after we moved in with them. —ANTHONY

My dad is a little strict with my stepbrothers. I don't think it's really fair. He's stricter with them than he is with me. —PAUL

Usually Alex, my stepsister, wants to call me from her mom's house, but her mom says no. That's unfair for Alex and me. Her mom guards the phone so Alex won't call me. Her mom is jealous of the fact that Alex and I get along with each other. —ETHAN

As a stepkid, you're likely dealing with parents and stepparents who don't agree on a lot of things. That may be because they look at life differently. For example, your dad may think kids should focus on doing what they love at school and not worry too much about grades. On the other hand, your stepmom might think it's really important to get good grades. Or your mom might believe that it's not that important to keep your home neat, while your stepdad may want everyone to clean as often as possible.

The adults around you might also have different ideas about how to spend money. This might be because they have different kinds of jobs, or no job at all. For example, your mom and stepdad may make a lot of money and buy things often. Meanwhile, your dad might be out of work right now and not as willing to spend money.

In addition, your parents and stepparents may come from really different backgrounds. Your mom may have grown up in a family where she was taught that kids need to play and have fun. Meanwhile, your stepdad may have grown up in a strict family that focused on work, work, and more work.

This chapter is packed with advice about how to think about—and deal with—the different ways your parents and stepparents look at the world and treat you and your stepsiblings. You'll learn about the importance of understanding other points of view, and you might even gain a new perspective about what's "fair."

Seven Things Adults in Stepfamilies Might Disagree About

Let's look at some of the things the adults in your life may not see eye-to-eye about:

1. How much money to spend on you and your stepsiblings

2. What rules to set for you and your stepsiblings (about screen time, phone time, table manners, chores, homework, bedtime, and more)

3. How much time you should spend with your parent, stepparent, or stepsiblings

4. What you should do after school

5. What kind of life you should lead

6. What kind of school you and your stepsiblings should attend

7. How to make the "visiting kids" (those who don't live there all the time) feel at home

Why should you care about all the things adults disagree about? When the adults in your life disagree or have different views, life can feel unfair for you at times. Your stepsiblings may get more toys, books, and video games than you do. However, you may get to spend more time with your mom or dad. What's fair in this case? Who gets the better deal?

Here's an example: You're a 10-year-old living with your mom, stepdad, and stepsister. Your 10-year-old stepsister gets to play video games, but you don't. Your mom thinks you should spend your time doing other things, like reading. She takes you to a bookstore once a week and spends an hour or so there reading with you. Your stepsister doesn't get to do this because her dad doesn't have time to read and doesn't want to spend money on books. But your stepsister would like her dad to read with her more. What's fair? Who gets the better deal?

What's Fair?

In this exercise, you get to be the judge. You're going to "hear" some cases in Stepfamily Court. Look at the "big picture" and then determine what's fair and unfair.

the big picture: (noun) looking at the "big picture" means looking at all the facts together, not just one fact all by itself.

Mia's Stepsisters Get More Birthday Gifts

The charge: Mia's stepsisters get more gifts on their birthdays than Mia does.

Fact: It's true that Mia's stepsisters get more gifts.

Fact: Mia's stepdad likes the table to be piled high with gifts on his daughters' birthdays.

Fact: In order to have a big pile of presents, Mia's stepdad buys his kids lots of little things, like boxes of markers and super balls. He buys some of these things for Mia, too, but not as many as he buys for his kids.

Fact: Mia's mom doesn't like buying lots of little presents. She likes to buy one or two big ones that the kids will have longer—like a model airplane or a pair of ice skates. She buys a couple of big gifts for Mia and a couple of big gifts for her stepdaughters.

Fact: Mia's mom and stepdad spend the same amount of money on each child for their birthdays.

One possible judgment
Given that Mia's mom and stepdad view birthdays differently, it seems that they've done a pretty good job of being fair. They each get to keep their own gift-giving style, and they spend the same amount of money on each child.

You be the judge
After reviewing the charge and facts of this case, what's your opinion? Do you agree with the judgment? Explain why or why not in your Survival Log.

Justin's Stepbrother Goes to a Private School— and Justin Doesn't

The charge: Justin goes to a big public school, while Justin's stepbrother, Dominic, goes to a smaller, private school where he gets more individual attention.

Fact: Justin gets to take extra classes during the summer and after school, where he gets lots of additional help from teachers.

Fact: Justin has his own computer and takes an online accelerated math class.

Fact: Justin is doing well in his public school. However, Dominic is a different person with unique needs and learning styles. Justin's stepparent is afraid Dominic will feel lost in a big school.

Fact: Justin's parents think it makes more sense to invest in a computer and extra classes for Justin than to enroll him in a private school.

One possible judgment

Because a small, private school works well for one kid, and public school with lots of extra activities works for the other child, this situation actually seems fair, even though it appears unfair on the surface. It may be that Justin wouldn't like attending a school like Dominic's, just as Dominic may not feel as comfortable as Justin does in public school.

You be the judge

You may or may not agree with the judgment. Do you think it's fair that Dominic goes to a private school, while Justin doesn't? Take a moment to write your opinion in your Survival Log.

Keisha Says She's Treated Like Cinderella

My mom died when I was four. My dad immediately married a woman who had two daughters my age. From that moment on, I felt like Cinderella. My stepmom took my stepsisters shopping for clothes and never took me. She made me do lots of chores, while my stepsisters didn't have to do as much. —KEISHA

The charge: Keisha is treated unfairly by her stepmom and expected to do too many chores.

Fact: Keisha's stepmom takes her own daughters shopping for clothes and doesn't take Keisha. Sometimes Keisha's dad gives Keisha money for clothes but rarely takes her shopping.

Fact: Keisha's stepmom asks Keisha to clean up more often than she asks her own kids to.

Fact: Keisha's dad does not ask his wife to treat all the kids equally.

One possible judgment

Keisha is being treated unfairly. She might want to pull some of the survival tools from her backpack and talk to her father about how her stepmom is treating her. If that doesn't work, she can talk directly to her stepmom. She might also talk with someone she trusts outside the family, like a teacher or counselor.

Uncovering new facts about the situation

After Keisha speaks to her dad or stepmom, she may uncover these additional facts:

New Fact: Keisha's stepmom is afraid that Keisha doesn't want to go shopping with her. She doesn't know how to ask her about this.

New Fact: Keisha's stepmom is open to changing who does what chores. She thinks she is dividing up the chores equally because Keisha lives full-time at their home, while her stepsisters live there only part-time.

New Fact: Keisha's dad is not aware that Keisha feels she is being treated unfairly.

You be the judge

Now that you've learned some new facts, what's your opinion? Take a moment to write it in your Survival Log.

When Some Kids Live Part-Time at Your Home—and You're There More Often

In many stepfamilies, like Keisha's, some kids live full-time at one place, while other kids live there part-time. This can create some problems. Let's look at Lin's case. He says his stepdad goes too far to make his daughter (Lin's stepsister, Maddy) feel at home.

My stepfather is so worried about making sure my stepsister feels at home. He goes way too far. If she wants to take a shower, he tells everyone else to get out so she'll have enough hot water. If she wants to have friends over, he asks everyone else to leave the house so she and her friends can have it to themselves. This is unfair to the rest of us. —LIN

Lin decides to talk to his mom about the situation. Afterwards, he realizes he needs to look at the big picture:

The charge: Lin's stepdad favors his daughter, Maddy, over his stepkids.

Fact: Lin's stepsister, Maddy, spends only one day a week at Lin's home.

Fact: Maddy doesn't always feel comfortable at Lin's home because she's not there very often. Also, she's shy and quiet.

Fact: Maddy's mother makes it clear she doesn't want Maddy to enjoy herself at Lin's home. That puts Maddy in a difficult situation.

Fact: Lin's stepdad would like to see Maddy more often, and he worries she won't want to visit anymore.

Lin's judgment

Okay, his stepdad goes overboard to make Maddy feel comfortable, but his intentions aren't bad. He's not trying to hurt Lin or the other kids. He's just worried about his daughter and shows it in ways that are a little annoying to the rest of the kids. Maybe Lin should cut his stepdad a little slack, or even talk to him about how Lin and the others can help Maddy feel more at home.

You be the judge

Do you agree with Lin's judgment? Why or why not?

Now that you've tried your hand at judging other kids' situations, think about your own stepfamily. In your Survival Log, write down your "charges" about what you think is unfair. Then gather facts about the big picture and write them down. Has your opinion changed? Have you come up with new ways to handle the situation?

Step-Tween Survival Tip

If you think you're not being treated fairly, you should feel the person out, and wait a little bit. Things might get better. If they don't get better, talk to your dad or mom and try to work things out. —*PAUL*

✓ Reality Check:
If You're Sure You're Being Treated Unfairly

You've gathered the facts and looked at the big picture. You've waited a little and hoped things would get better, but they haven't. You still feel like you're being treated unfairly. And the reality is, maybe you are. Perhaps a parent or stepparent really is favoring a sibling or stepsibling over you, giving him or her more privileges, and giving you more than your share of responsibilities. Whatever the reason for this, it is not okay. You deserve equal and fair treatment in your home. Period.

So what do you do? First, review all of your survival tools. Then, talk to your parent or your stepparent, if you feel comfortable. Otherwise, find a school counselor, teacher, grandparent, or other relative—someone you trust. You might say to a teacher, "I'm wondering if I could talk with you about something personal. I'm having a hard time with my stepfamily right now, and I'm looking for help. I feel like my stepmom treats me unfairly and I'm not sure how to talk to her or my dad about it."

Stepping Closer

Is your birthday coming up? Before you set the date for your family celebration, check with your stepsiblings to make sure they'll be available. Let them know it wouldn't feel like a party without them. If you check in with them about this, they'll feel like they're important—and being treated "fairly."

CHAPTER 9

When Your Stepdad Wears His Undershirt to the Breakfast Table...and Other Uncomfortable Moments

 ## Stepkids Speak Out

Sometimes my mom and stepdad try to make everyone act like a family. We all go out together. It doesn't feel comfortable with my stepdad. My mom will be in between me and my stepdad. We'll both be talking to her and not to each other. It feels weird. —OLIVIA

> *When we're on vacation and sharing a bathroom, I don't like it when my stepbrother sees my underwear. I always try to hide them from him, and when he sees them, I feel so embarrassed. It's awful.* —SAMANTHA
>
> *It's weird having a new guy, my stepdad, live with us. I just met my stepdad and I haven't gotten to know him. It would feel better if I had more time to get to know him before living with him.* —PAIGE

Like Olivia, Samantha, and Paige, you may find yourself in some situations that make you feel uncomfortable in your stepfamily. Does your stepdad arrive at the breakfast table in his workout clothes—a stinky tank top and gym shorts? Does your stepmom wear a Hawaiian-style dress imprinted with topless Hula girls? What about your stepgrandparents? Do they practically soak your face when they're kissing you hello?

You're now living in close quarters with people you may not know well, yet. It's likely you'll feel uncomfortable at times. You'll learn in this chapter how to identify what feels okay and not-so-okay to you. You'll also get more practice communicating your feelings.

It's fine if you don't want to see your steprelatives in their underwear or have them breathing in your face or invading your bedroom. It's also fine if they don't feel like your family yet.

Stepkids Speak Out

> *My new stepbrother's bedroom was in the family room because we didn't have enough bedrooms. Once he was in his boxers. It was like, "Eww!" It felt pretty weird and I was too embarrassed to say anything.* —CHLOE

Know Yourself:
How Would You Feel If Your
Stepbrother Shared Too Much
of Himself?

Let's say you're a girl in Chloe's situation. Your stepbrother lounges in his boxers in the living room. You sometimes see more than you ever needed or asked to see of his body. How would you feel?

Choose all the answers that apply to you.

* Embarrassed or ashamed
* Angry at him for being so crude
* Nervous and uncomfortable
* Slightly annoyed
* Totally amused
* Really shocked and upset
* Tempted to tease him
* Completely unfazed by the whole thing

Whether you chose one, three, or all of these responses—you're not alone. All the responses are typical for some people. What's most important is that you know how you feel. Consider what makes you comfortable or uncomfortable. Think about what makes you feel like your space has been invaded or your line has been crossed.

Where Do You Draw the Line?

Following are some examples of other stepkids "drawing the line" between feeling comfortable and uncomfortable:

1. I feel comfortable when my stepmom hugs me goodnight, but I feel like she's invading my space when she kisses me goodnight.

2. I feel comfortable when my stepbrother wears his jeans with no shirt, but I feel uncomfortable when he only wears his boxers around the house.

3. I feel comfortable eating breakfast with my stepsister, but I feel uncomfortable when she sits there and stares at me without smiling.

4. I feel comfortable when my sister comes into my room without knocking, but I feel like my space is invaded when my stepsister does it.

5. I like to chat with my stepdad, but I don't like it when he gets really close to me and talks in my face and I can smell his breath.

6. Now, add a few "comfortables" and "uncomfortables" of your own in your Survival Log.

Watch for Signs That Your Line Has Been Crossed

You probably know when you feel uncomfortable. You feel it in your heart, head, palms, stomach, or underarms. You may begin to feel so warm that you're sure you have a fever. Sweat may begin pouring down your sides. Your heartbeat might pick up a little—or a lot. You may feel queasy in your stomach and a strong desire to get away.

Whatever you're feeling, there's probably a very good reason for it. It's important to pay attention to these warning signs.

What to Do When Someone in Your Stepfamily Makes You Feel Uncomfortable

You've got a few choices here. You might want to talk to your parent first or directly to the person who's bugging you. If you start with your parent, here are some examples of things to say:

Three things you might say to your parent

1. "Mom, it makes me feel uncomfortable when my stepdad invites his card buddies over and asks them to hug me."

2. "Dad, I don't like it when my stepmom stands really close to me when she's talking. I feel like she's invading my space."

3. "Mom, I feel uncomfortable when my stepbrother gives me a mean look every time I come into the room."

Three things you might say to your steprelative

1. To your stepdad: "I'm sure your friends are nice, but I don't know them very well. I feel uncomfortable when they hug me."

2. To your stepmom, "Can you please take a few steps back so I can see you better? It's hard for me to see you and listen to you when you're so close."

3. To your stepbrother, "I know it's hard to share a room. I'm not used to it, either. But it would help if you didn't look angry when I walk in the room. And if you are mad at me, can you please tell me why?"

Add statements that apply to your situation in your Survival Log.

Important! Whenever you feel those warning bells in your head, heart, armpits, or stomach, communicate them. Find a safe, trusted adult who will listen to you if the people around you aren't listening or if you're still feeling uncomfortable.

What If You Want to Get Closer?

We've talked about what happens when your stepfamily members get too close to you and make you feel icky. But what if your new stepsibling is really cute and you want to get closer to her or him?

This actually is a common situation. Step-tweens and teens often feel excited and curious when they're developing new relationships in stepfamilies. There's nothing wrong with you if you feel this way. It can be normal for stepkids to have crushes on one another. Your friends may even be telling you just how cute your stepsibling is! They may even suggest that you act on the crush. However, experts and other stepkids will tell you this isn't a good idea. Why? Even if you don't feel like it yet, your stepsibling is part of your family now.

In time, there's a good chance your stepbrother or stepsister won't seem so cute to you. As you get to know each other better and spend time together as a family, your stepsibling will probably just feel like another family member—not someone you'd want to take to the prom!

You might want to talk to a parent, stepparent, teacher, or counselor about your feelings toward your stepsibling— or write them down in your Survival Log.

Reality Check:
If You Feel Scared or Unsafe

Some situations will make unusually loud warning bells go off inside you. Pay attention to them. Loud warning bells will go off if people in your stepfamily try to see or touch the private parts of your body. They'll also go off if people ask you to touch or see their private parts, or if they hit you or threaten you. If something feels uncomfortable to you, it doesn't matter if other people say it's okay. *It's not.*

If you're dealing with a situation like this, talk to your parent. If that doesn't work, or you don't feel comfortable doing that, talk to another trusted adult. This could be a grandparent, aunt, uncle, teacher, school counselor, or spiritual leader. Don't give up! Keep talking until you find someone who will listen and help. You might begin by saying, "This is hard for me to say, but I don't feel comfortable when my stepdad touches me in certain ways. Can you help me?"

Step-Tween Survival Tip

When I was feeling really powerless and trapped, it helped me to go to a community center near where I lived and get counseling. I also found a trusted adult who I could tell everything to—a teacher. —*JONATHAN*

Stepping Closer

Are you feeling like your stepsister is invading your space? Sometimes airing your feelings can make you feel closer to someone. Let 'em out! Ask her to go on a walk or toss a ball with you and say something like, "Can we both agree to knock first before opening each other's bedroom doors? I don't know how you handle surprise, but I practically jump out of my chair when that door flings open and I'm not expecting it." She'll likely be glad you told her.

CHAPTER 10

Your Parents Haven't Forgotten About You, But It Might Feel That Way

Stepkids Speak Out

For a long time, I was alone with my mom. Then we moved in with my stepdad and his kids, and I was worried my mom would pay more attention to my stepsiblings than me. I worried they'd get more presents on holidays, and I wouldn't be important. —ANTHONY

My stepmom at first did not want to deal with me and my two siblings. She and my dad had a new baby and it was clear they didn't want to have us kids around. —JONATHAN

> *It was really a big deal when my mom and stepdad had a baby. Everyone would come over all the time and look at the baby.* —OLIVIA

Like Anthony, you may have had your mom or dad all to yourself until one (or both) of them found a new partner. You may have been the one your parents always turned to for advice or help. Maybe you got used to going shopping or to the movies alone with your parent.

Then, you got a stepparent, maybe a couple of stepsiblings, or even a new baby sister or brother. Suddenly, your mom or dad got busier than ever. Suddenly, Mom or Dad seemed too busy even for you.

In this situation, it's easy to feel ignored or to worry that your parent won't have enough time for you. You'll read in this chapter about ideas for communicating that you feel rejected or left out. You'll also find tips for trying to improve your situation.

First of all, it's important to understand that your parents love you and haven't forgotten about you. Your mom and stepdad—or dad and stepmom—are probably hoping to create a happy family for you by bringing these people into your life. Right now, your parent is also trying to get to know all the new family members, which might make you feel left out. Your parent may be working really hard to make everyone feel at home in your stepfamily. That probably leaves less time for you.

Remember: Chances are, your parent is not choosing one person over another or favoring anyone over you. Your parent is trying to bring two families together and get acquainted with new family members, just like you are.

Know Yourself:
Check Your
Feeling Left Out-O-Meter

Let's take a look at how you react when you're feeling like everyone forgot about you.

Respond to the following items by rating your feelings on a scale from 1 to 6. Write the rating for each item in your Survival Log.

1 = I never feel this way.
3 = I sometimes feel this way.
6 = I always feel this way.

FEELING LEFT OUT-O-METER

A) When I feel like my mom or dad ignores me, I:

want to get away and hide. 1 **2 3 4 5 6**

hang around and ask lots of questions. 1 **2 3 4 5 6**

throw temper tantrums about little things—
like how my parent cooks dinner 1 **2 3 4 5 6**

feel angry and yell a lot 1 **2 3 4 5 6**

B) When I see my mom spending lots of time with my stepdad, I:

stick myself between them and hug my mom. 1 **2 3 4 5 6**

do cartwheels or other stunts to get my
mom's attention 1 **2 3 4 5 6**

say mean things to my stepdad, like "I hate you!"
and hope he'll go away 1 **2 3 4 5 6**

tell my mom that my stepdad is boring and dumb. 1 **2 3 4 5 6**

C) When my dad plays with the new baby instead of me, I:

wish the baby would go back to the hospital 1 **2 3 4 5 6**

do back flips in front of my dad so he'll look at me 1 **2 3 4 5 6**

sit on my dad's lap when he's trying to cuddle
with the baby. 1 **2 3 4 5 6**

If you chose 4, 5, or 6 more than five times, read on. If you're often tempted to do back flips or throw temper tantrums to get your mom's or dad's attention, it's time to sit down and think about what you're missing. What would make you feel better?

Four Things That Might Make You Feel Better

What exactly is it about your old family that you miss? Close your eyes and imagine doing some of the things that you miss most. What comes to mind? Here are some examples to get you started:

1. I'd like my mom to cook my favorite spaghetti-smothered-in-butter dinner. (She never makes it anymore because my stepdad thinks it will make his kids fat.)

2. I'd like to go to the library with my dad once a week like we used to. But now he's busy taking care of my younger stepsiblings.

3. I want to watch a movie with my mom without anyone interrupting.

4. I'd like my dad to spend more time helping me with my homework.

Now it's your turn. Add at least four of your own ideas in your Survival Log.

It looks like time for some Straight Talk with your parent. Be sure to find a good time to talk. For example, don't try to talk to your mom if:

a) She looks like she hasn't slept in five days.
b) The baby is screaming.
c) Your golden retriever just chewed a hole in the living room couch.
d) Your stepdad's ex-wife just appeared on your doorstep for the first time.

In the above cases, your mom is probably very busy coping. Wait a little before talking—maybe until later in the day or tomorrow.

Remember, using Straight Talk and I-messages won't always get you what you want right away. But they can help you explain how you feel. That's an important start.

Three Things You Could Say to Your Parent When You Feel Ignored

1. "Mom, I know you have a lot on your hands right now with our new stepfamily. But I miss our time together. Could I sometimes spend time with just you alone, like we used to do?"

2. "Dad, I know babies need a lot of attention, but I'm feeling left out. I wish we could spend more time together playing catch like we used to."

3. "Mom, when I see you playing with my stepbrother, I get jealous. I keep worrying that you're going to love him more than me. I just want you to know that's how I feel sometimes."

Write a list of your own requests or feelings in your Survival Log.

 ## Step-Tween Survival Tip

It's a good idea to stick up for what you want. Even if you're shy, try to figure out a way to speak up. —ETHAN

Understanding What's Normal in Stepfamilies

"But I tried my best Straight Talk, and my dad was so busy tickling the baby, he didn't even hear me," you might say. "Before I tried to talk to him, I felt like the Rapidly Disappearing Kid. Now I feel totally invisible! What do I do?"

Try to look at the big picture. The way you're feeling is probably pretty common for kids in new stepfamilies. It can be normal when:

* You miss the time you spent alone with your parent before the remarriage or new partnership.

* You feel like you've been replaced by your new stepparent.

* Your parent finds a new partner or spouse and acts all mushy and in love (don't worry—they probably won't act this way forever!).

* There's a new baby at home who needs lots of time and energy.

* Your parent is stressed, worried, or really busy because everything is so new and different in your family.

* There's a lot of confusion about who's going to spend time with who and how often.

You may feel like you're the only one who ever felt left out by a parent who recently remarried, had a baby, or both. But you're definitely not alone! In every kid's life, parents may be too busy, stressed, or distracted to give kids their full attention all the time. Usually this happens when something big is going on in the family. The birth of a baby, a divorce, a new marriage or partnership, a new job, a new home, an illness, or a death are all big family events. Whether for happy or sad reasons, adults just don't always have the time or energy to give kids their complete attention.

Do you have a friend whose parents remarried, had a baby, or experienced some other big change at home? This friend probably has already felt what you're going through. Most friends really want to help, especially when their buddy is having a tough day, or week, or month. Why not ask how your friend got through it? You never know what you might learn.

Five Questions to Ask Friends About Parents Getting Remarried or Having Babies

1. After your parents remarried, moved in with a new partner, or had a baby, did they spend as much time with you as they used to?

2. How did you feel when all of this happened? Were you sad? Confused? Okay about it?

3. Did you tell anyone how you were feeling? Who did you tell? Did it help?

4. What if you needed help with your homework or you wanted to watch a movie with your mom, but she was too busy? What did you do?

5. How are things now? Did things get better?

No one has all the answers. Each family and situation is different. Asking friends for advice can be helpful because you may hear ideas you never thought of. Just remember: Other people's ideas may not work for you. But asking people close to you for suggestions or help or just to lend an ear—"Talk with an Adult You Trust"—is a great tool in your survival backpack.

 **Step-Tween Survival Tip**

I talk to my friends all the time. They just listen. It's really helpful to have friends who will listen. —*OLIVIA*

Let 'Em Out

If you'd rather not talk to friends, you might feel better putting your thoughts and feelings on paper. Express yourself in a journal. Draw a self-portrait that shows your mood, and then draw another one in a month to see how your mood has changed. You might even create a "wish list" of things you'd like to happen in your new family. Share it with your parent and stepparent, or a counselor, to let them know what's on your mind.

Imagine Your Future

Take a minute to close your eyes. Imagine how you'd like to feel in your stepfamily.

In your Survival Log, write a scene for a movie or book about how life might be in the future, when things have settled down and you're feeling less invisible. Your script might read something like this:

I just woke up to the sound of my stepdad making my favorite breakfast. He made me pancakes and fresh orange juice. We feel happy and comfortable with each other. And there's my baby sister. She's two now. All she wants to do is get up on my bed and stare at me, admire me, touch me. The best part of all: She laughs at all my jokes, even when she doesn't get them! Here comes my stepbrother. He gives me a high-five and winks at me, like we've known each other forever. "See you at school," he says, and I realize I'm excited to see him there. It's fun having a stepbrother in the same grade as me, especially since I never had a brother before. The other kids have lots of questions and are always trying to figure out if we act alike, if we have the same talents, or like the same things.

Did you write something similar in your Survival Log? You never know, some of it just might come true. Read what kids who've been there have to say:

The Good News from Stepkids

I like having so many parents, stepparents, and siblings. The more, the merrier. I even wish my mom would have another baby sometime. I also wish I could spend more time with my stepsiblings, outside of their schedules. It's more fun when there are more people around. —ETHAN

Having a baby sister, is, well, you know, not that bad. You have someone who looks up to you. —OLIVIA

At first, all my stepbrother did was try to get my attention. Now he's like a brother to me. I always introduce him to my friends as my brother. —ANTHONY

Reality Check: If You're Still Feeling Left Out in the Cold

Maybe you feel like quotes about a happy stepfamily don't apply to you. Tell your parents what's on your mind, or show them this section of the book. Let them know exactly how you feel. If you're not comfortable talking about this with a parent, talk to someone else you trust—maybe an aunt, an uncle, or a grandparent. Chances are this person has also felt rejected or ignored at some point in his or her life. You might start by saying, "Grandpa, do you have time to talk? I'm feeling really left out at home, like my dad and stepmom have forgotten all about me, and I'm hoping you can help me out by listening."

Step-Tween Survival Tip

My grandparents were so important to me. I was able to stay in touch with them, write them, and call them. I also had an aunt I got really close to. I managed to keep a sense of family this way. —*JONATHAN*

Stepping Closer

Are you feeling as if your parents aren't paying much attention to you? You might want to spend time with your stepsibling, if you have one. Is your stepbrother really good at graphic design? Does your stepsister play field hockey for her high school team? Ask them about their talents and hobbies. How did they learn them? Why do they like them? You might even ask them to teach you something.

CHAPTER II

Moving Forward with Trust, Hope, and Plenty of Survival Skills

 ## Stepkids Speak Out

I felt like it was my fault my parents were getting a divorce. All of a sudden they started fighting, and I thought it was something I did. —ZIAD

Why me? I think that all the time. Why me? Why did this happen to me? —SUN

You have this hurt from your parents splitting up and so many emotions swirling around. Try to understand that it's not your responsibility. The divorce was something that was imposed on you. —ANNA

Like Sun, you might feel alone and wonder why you're the one whose parents divorced and remarried. You might ask yourself over and over, "Why me? Did I do something wrong? Was it my fault?" You're definitely not the only stepkid who feels this way. In this final chapter, you'll read stories and tips from other step-tweens about how they learned to thrive in their stepfamilies, in spite of the challenges.

Remember, kids can't make their parents get divorced or remarried because of things they say or do. It was not your fault. If you find yourself asking, "Why did this happen to me?" it may be helpful to remind yourself that you're not alone. Millions of kids and teens currently live in stepfamilies. In fact, more than half of all Americans are now in a stepfamily or will be part of one sometime during their lives.

As the stepkids quoted in this book have said, it's not always easy being in a stepfamily. Many kids don't like it when stepparents try to push new rules on them. They aren't always comfortable having people who feel like strangers living in their home. They often miss the parent they don't get to see very often. They may also feel lost, left out, or forgotten sometimes.

The Good Stuff About Stepkids

Kids who live in stepfamilies often grow up to be flexible, accepting, and tolerant (which means they're open to new kinds of people and things). These are great traits! Stepkids learn many important life skills, like how to get along and communicate with divorced parents, stepparents, and stepsiblings. They learn how to talk to other people who may like different things and behave very differently than they do.

Yes, being in a stepfamily can be a challenge, especially at first. But you can rise to this challenge and even discover the good in your situation.

How Can You Rise to the Challenge?

Read the following quotes and stories, and consider how they might apply to you.

Life's challenges are not supposed to paralyze you, they're supposed to help you discover who you are. —BERNICE JOHNSON REAGON, AFRICAN-AMERICAN HISTORIAN AND MUSICIAN

Don't always wait until everything is just right. It will never be perfect. There will always be challenges, obstacles and less than perfect conditions. So what? Get started now. With each step you take, you will grow stronger and stronger, more and more skilled, more and more self-confident and more and more successful. —MARK VICTOR HANSEN, COAUTHOR OF CHICKEN SOUP FOR THE SOUL

I have always grown from my problems and challenges, from the things that don't work out. That's when I've really learned. —CAROL BURNETT, COMEDIAN, ACTRESS, SINGER, AND DANCER

How Jonathan Made the Best of a Not-So-Great Situation

Jonathan didn't like leaving his friends and pets behind to move to a new city and live with a new family. He didn't like the fact that his stepdad tried to force him to call him "Dad." He had trouble with the fact that his stepdad was totally in charge of the family, and Jonathan's mother did not support Jonathan and his siblings.

To get through high school, Jonathan learned how to reach out. He reached out to his grandmother, aunts, and uncles. He also became close to one of his English teachers. These people supported Jonathan and gave him advice.

→

"I reached out and people responded. If someone didn't respond, I'd move on to someone else," Jonathan says. He also learned how to care for himself and his younger sister, who he picked up at school every day.

Rather than focusing only on his troubles, Jonathan put his troubles to work for him. He used his sense of humor and writing skills. He kept a journal and eventually turned his life story into a published book.

As an adult, Jonathan helped create a comedy show about his life that runs at nightclubs in five U.S. cities. During the show, Jonathan and six others read from their journals. He has even told his story on a popular national radio show.

What's more, Jonathan created an after-school program for middle school children to study art and literature and to help them find counselors if they want to talk to a professional about their feelings. The program is used in four Los Angeles schools.

Jonathan especially enjoys helping kids who are experiencing family troubles like he did. "Because of my experiences, I can listen to the kids. I don't judge them. They can really share their feelings with me," he says.

How Jake Applies Stepfamily Lessons to His Everyday Life

"I've gone through so much in my parents' divorce and remarriage, I feel like I can get through anything," says Jake, now a high school student and captain of his soccer team.

Getting to know his stepmom, stepdad, and stepsiblings was one of Jake's biggest challenges at first. He tried his best to understand what made each of them happy, sad, or angry. He now uses the lessons he learned about understanding people in all aspects of his life. "It's helped me learn how to live life successfully, without a lot of conflict," he says. His stepfamily experience also helped him understand the importance of listening. He's quick to listen to a friend who's troubled.

In addition, Jake learned how to hang in there when times get tough. "I'm definitely a stronger person. You get a lot of life lessons from being in a stepfamily. You have a 'one-up' on everyone else," he says. For example, Jake gained excellent communication skills that help him get along with many of the people in his life—including friends, girlfriends, teachers, and coaches. "That's a great advantage in life," he says.

How Chloe Moved Forward

Chloe's mom died when Chloe was a kid. A year later, her dad remarried. His new wife and two kids moved in. Chloe didn't like sharing her room with a stepsister who had such different tastes. She didn't like having a stepbrother living in the family room. Even though Chloe was sad about losing her mother, she learned to use her sense of humor as often as possible in her new family. She found ways to be flexible and to understand other people's points of view. At the same time, she discovered that she should insist on doing things "her way" if it felt important enough to her. "I learned to be true to myself. I had my own style, taste, and morals," she says.

Chloe now works as a nanny, and believes her experiences in a stepfamily help her bring flexibility, humor, and empathy to her work.

empathy: (noun) the ability to see someone else's point of view

Chloe's advice:

* Be clear about what you want and need in your personal space—your bedroom, for example.

* Try to be flexible about changes in your home, including furniture and chores.

* Be sure to laugh, because it will often make you feel better.

* Don't make fun of those around you. It could come back to haunt you.

* Remember that your parent is your ally—on your side—in your family.

Five Ways to Make the Best of Your Stepfamily Situation

1. When things get tough, trust that life will get better. Go with the flow when if feels comfortable for you. Also, be sure to believe in yourself. That's what Jake did, but it wasn't easy at first.

2. Express your anger, sadness, confusion, excitement, or frustration by writing, singing, or drawing. That's what Jonathan and Chloe did.

3. Even if it's difficult, stick your neck out and say what you feel (using Straight Talk and your other survival tools). The more you do this, the better you'll be at it. Like Jonathan did, reach out to those around you.

4. Laugh at your situation when you can. Make jokes about the parts of your stepfamily life that may be funny or unexpected (just be careful not to make fun of family members). Write comedy routines or share some stories with your closest friends. Jake, Jonathan, and Chloe all learned how to use their sense of humor during challenging times.

5. Ask for help when you need it! Seek out a friend or an adult you know and trust. Most people really like to feel needed by those they care about. They are usually happy to listen or help when asked.

Now it's your turn. In your Survival Log, write down four ways that you could rise to the challenges in your stepfamily— and even learn and grow from them.

Step-Tween Survival Tips

I found three or four people who were helpful. They mostly stayed in touch with me and listened. That grounded me and helped me feel like part of a family.
—*JONATHAN*

People told me life in a stepfamily would get better. And it did. No, it's not perfect, but it's a big step from where I came from. It's never going to be perfect. Even if my parents were still married, it would not be perfect. You need to take life as it is given to you. Roll with the punches. Trust it will get better. —*JAKE*

Take Out Your Survival Gear

You've now got the tools you need to express your feelings and improve your situation. Keep this book handy so you can pull out a helpful tool, tip, reminder, or comforting quote when you need one.

Step-Tween Survival Tools

1. Let 'Em Out!
2. Talk with an Adult You Trust
3. Practice Straight Talk
4. Use I-Messages
5. Look for the Positives
6. Keep a Sense of Humor
7. Ask for What You Need
8. Brainstorm
9. Compromise & Negotiate

Using these tools, what can you say to let others know how you feel and what you need?

* How can you express yourself so people will listen?

* What can you do to feel happier and more comfortable in your home?

* What can you do to get to know the new people in your life?

* How can you get help if things aren't going well?

You have what it takes to tackle these questions, and more. It takes a lot of courage to deal with all the changes in your family and in your everyday life. But you have the power to express yourself and feel better. Keep reaching out to the people in your life who love and care about you. And remember: You are not alone, and you deserve to feel happy and hopeful.

Like Jonathan, Chloe, and Jake—and all the kids quoted in this book—you can learn a lot from the challenges and changes in your life. Soon, you too may have lots to say about how much stronger, wiser, and more flexible and capable you are as a result of your experiences in your stepfamily.

A Note to Parents and Stepparents

Living in a stepfamily can be joyful, but it can also be challenging. This is especially true for many tweens—kids roughly between the ages of 9 and 12. Developmentally, your tween's primary focus is to seek more independence and autonomy, develop an adolescent identity, pursue peer relationships, and meet the increasing demands of school and social life. Now, he or she is also faced with the task of learning to cope with a myriad of changes and transitions that accompany stepfamily life. It can be a lot to handle.

This book is intended to help your tween navigate the sometimes-rocky waters of stepfamily life by providing tools that promote effective communication and coping. Included are real-life examples, strategies, and activities to help tween readers express their needs and feelings, enhance relationships, address common challenges, and identify when (and how) to seek additional support.

How to Use This Book

This book is designed as a resource for kids. *But it's important that you read it, too.* You'll gain additional insight into some of the issues and challenges your child may be grappling with. Let her or him know that you're available to talk about the topics addressed in this book, and you're here to help.

Find regular opportunities to connect with your child and support the adjustment to the many changes in his or her family life. Make time for one-on-one activities, even if that sometimes means simply walking the dog or doing errands together. These moments can provide important opportunities for your child to ask questions, share feelings, and feel assured that you're attentive and available.

Recognize that your tween may be experiencing a range of emotions and getting to know new stepfamily members can take time. Be patient and supportive during this transition in your family.

While this book provides specific tools for kids in stepfamilies, it is not a substitute for professional advice. If you have questions or concerns about your child's mood, behaviors, or adjustment to stepfamily life, seek professional guidance.

Books to Check Out

The Bright Side: Surviving Your Parents' Divorce by Max Sindell (HCI Teens, 2007). Written for teens by an author who was recently a teen, this book is a fun, informative, honest account of dealing with your parents' divorce and stepfamily life. Includes a "Bill of Rights" for kids of divorce.

Let's Talk About It: Stepfamilies by Fred Rogers (Puffin, 2001). In clear simple language, this book helps you learn how to cope with change so you can find your place in your new family.

My Parents Are Divorced, Too: A Book for Kids by Kids (Second Edition) by Melanie, Annie, and Steven Ford (Magination Press, 2006). Three stepsiblings tell about their struggles and triumphs living through their parents' divorces. Includes original cartoon strips.

Stepliving for Teens: Getting Along with Stepparents and Siblings by Joel D. Block and Susan S. Bartell (Price Stern Sloan, 2001). This book explores a wide range of questions from real teens about life in a stepfamily, answered by two professionals who specialize in family relationships.

What in the World Do You Do When Your Parents Divorce? A Survival Guide for Kids by Kent Winchester and Roberta Beyer (Free Spirit Publishing, 2001). This little book is packed full of answers to common questions kids have about their parents' divorce, such as "Was it my fault?" "What happens to our family now?" "Will my parents ever get back together?" and "What do I do about my feelings?"

Web Sites to Check Out

It's My Life
http://pbskids.org/itsmylife

Whatever problem you're dealing with, believe it or not, other kids and
teens have gone through the same thing. On It's My Life, you can read
informative articles, share your stories, play games and activities, take
quizzes and polls, watch video clips of other kids talking about their
feelings and experiences, get advice from older kids and experts, and
contribute your own comments and questions.

KidsHealth
www.KidsHealth.org

KidsHealth is the largest and most-visited site on the Web providing
trusted health information for kids of all ages. Visit the Kids site and click
on "Dealing with Feelings" to find links to articles about stepfamilies under
"My Home & Family." Or, enter the Teens site and click on "Your Mind,"
where you'll find information on a variety of topics, including Parents
and Families.

Index

About the Authors

Lisa Cohn is an award-winning freelance writer and author. Her favorite part of her job is interviewing kids and adults like the ones she interviewed for this book. She also is the author of *One Family, Two Family, New Family: Stories and Advice for Stepfamilies*. Her articles have appeared in the *Christian Science Monitor*, *Mothering, Parenting, Brain, Child: The Magazine for Thinking Mothers*, and other publications. She is now working—along with her brother—on a book/CD program for kids in sports (and their parents).

Write to her and learn more by visiting www.stepfamilyadvice.com or www.youthsportspsychology.com. She lives in Oregon with her partner, two kids, and two stepkids.

Debbie Glasser, Ph.D., is a psychologist and writer who helps kids and parents in all kinds of families learn how to understand each other and get along better. She is a freelance parenting columnist for the *Miami Herald* and past chairperson of the National Parenting Education Network (NPEN). She also edits an online newsletter for parents and can be reached at www.NewsForParents.org.

Debbie lives in a stepfamily. Two of her three children, Emily and Ben, are stepkids. Debbie and her husband, Glenn, also have a son named Sam.

Other Great Books from Free Spirit!

Fighting Invisible Tigers
Stress Management for Tees (Revised & Updated Third Edition)
By Earl Hipp

Stress is something we all experience. But recent research suggests that adolescents are affected by it in unique ways that can increase impulsivity and risky behaviors. This book offers proven techniques that teens can use to deal with stressful situations in school, at home, and among friends. They'll find current information on how stress affects health and decision making and learn stress-management skills to handle stress in positive ways—including assertiveness, positive self-talk, time management, relaxation exercises, and much more.

$14.95, Softcover, 160 pp., 2-color illust., 6" x 9", for ages 11 & up

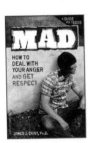

Mad
How to Deal with Your Anger and Get Respect
By James J. Crist, Ph.D.

Anger is a normal human emotion. But some teens have trouble controlling their anger and get into trouble with their parents, their school, or the law. This positive, supportive book is especially helpful for teens with anger control problems. Practical tools and strategies help them understand and handle their anger and avoid poor decisions and rash actions. Insights from real teens let readers know they're not alone. The final chapters explore mental health problems that can complicate anger management and consider the role of counseling and psychotherapy. Includes resources.

$13.95, Softcover, 160 pp., 2-color illust., 6" x 9", for ages 13 & up

Too Old for This, Too Young for That!
Your Survival Guide for the Middle-School Years
By Harriet S. Mosatche, Ph.D., and Karen Unger, M.A.

Comprehensive, interactive, friendly, and fun, this book tells "tweens" what they need to know to survive and thrive during middle school. Covers physical and emotional changes; family friends, and school; making decisions; handling peer pressure; setting and reaching goals; and preparing for the years ahead.

$14.95, Softcover, 200 pp., illust., 7" x 9", for ages 10–14

To place an order or to request a free catalog of
Self-Help for Kids® and Self-Help for Teens® materials,
please write, call, email, or visit our Web site:

Free Spirit Publishing Inc.
217 Fifth Avenue North • Suite 200 • Minneapolis, MN 55401-1299
toll-free 800.735.7323 • local 612.338.2038 • fax 612.337.5050
help4kids@freespirit.com • www.freespirit.com